DRAMA Across The CURRICULUM

THE FICTIONAL FAMILY IN PRACTICE

MURIEL GOLD, C.M., PH.D.

iUniverse, Inc.
New York   Bloomington

Drama Across the Curriculum
The Fictional Family in Practice

iUniverse books may be ordered through booksellers or by contacting:

iUniverse
1663 Liberty Drive
Bloomington, IN 47403
www.iuniverse.com
1-800-Authors (1-800-288-4677)

ISBN: 978-1-4502-4071-0 (pbk)
ISBN: 978-1-4502-4072-7 (ebk)

Printed in the United States of America

iUniverse rev. date: 8/5/10

For my real and fictional families

Suddenly she felt a great urge to become someone else, one of those passers-by walking through the snow, for example. Her deepest desire was to live in some other place than within herself, for just a minute, one brief minute, to see what it is like inside a head other than her own, another body, to be incarnated anew, to know what it is like in some other place, to know new sorrows, new joys, to try on a different skin from her own, the way one tries on gloves in a store, to stop gnawing on the one bone of her actual life and feed on strange, disorienting substances…to inhabit profoundly another being with all the knowledge, the compassion, the sense of rootedness, the efforts to adapt and the strange and fearsome mystery that would entail.

Anne Hébert (1990)

Foreword

Dorothy Heathcote, the groundbreaking and influential drama educator, once explained that she used her original theatre background in her current work as an educator by placing theatre principles at the service of students' learning.

> A lot of people think that if you work in improvisation, then you don't work in theatre. Of course you work in theatre. One of the ways you make the ideas work is you understand how the theatre works, how it exposes the ideas that lie between people...The theatre's in my blood. I have a lot of understanding about it...And I use that expertise for the children, not for theatre. (1971)

The work of Heathcote and a number of her colleagues in Britain helped move improvisational drama beyond the isolated realm of the drama specialist (usually in a special room at a special time) into the mainstream of the school curriculum by developing it as another—and powerful— means of teaching and learning in the classroom, along with discussion, reading, writing, visual media, and so on. Thus, today there is a clearly defined field referred to as "drama in education" (as opposed to "drama education") and phrases such as "drama as a learning medium" and "drama for learning" are relatively common. This shift in the role and place of drama in schooling paralleled the development of the Language Across the Curriculum movement which encouraged teachers to consider how learners' language use, both oral and written, could be used in more powerful and effective ways for learning in all curricular areas. Drama in education provided another aspect of students' language use which could be a means of learning across the curriculum, in this case using understandings and techniques from the world of theatre.

I've started my foreword with this brief historical perspective because this current volume represents and extends this tradition of drama in education with roots in the world of theatre. More particularly, I focused on the unique contributions of Dorothy Heathcote, originally an actor, because of striking parallels between her orientation and that of Muriel Gold, upon whose work this volume is based. Like Heathcote, Gold's origins, and current strengths, are in the theatre, as exhibited by a long and distinguished career as actor, director, and artistic director. And like Heathcote, Gold also became an educator, first as a teacher of acting and theatre arts. In this capacity she developed over a number of years an approach to actor's training which she calls The Fictional Family. That approach to teaching acting is well and fully described in her earlier book (1991) by the same name. Yet Gold is an educator in a broader sense, having used her Fictional Family techniques in a wide range of educational contexts, purposes, and audiences, including teachers who have learned to use her techniques as a teaching and learning tool in their own subject areas. This edited volume is important since it collects for the first time descriptions of a number of applications of the Fictional Family technique for purposes of fostering students' learning across a range of subject areas, from writing to history, and for various cross-curricular themes, such as multicultural education and gender issues. As such, this volume serves as a companion to her earlier book and will be of most interest to secondary and post-secondary educators.

The volume begins with a brief introduction to the technique and a general orientation to its use across the curriculum. Yet the heart of the volume is a number of detailed descriptions of the technique in use as a teaching and learning tool by Gold herself, but also by other teachers in their subject areas. This is not an instructional book, with a set of detailed steps to follow in order to use the technique in your own teaching. Rather it forms a constellation of the creative uses of the flexible protocol that is the Fictional Family, told in the voices of several gifted teachers. As such, I find it inspiring and instructive as I continue to imagine my own possible uses of the technique. Yet the real power of the volume may lie elsewhere. To get to that point, please follow me on a brief digression.

I recently had an opportunity to do some improvised drama with a grade 5 class in a local school. My efforts were observed by the children's regular teacher as well as the school's resource teacher who frequently worked in the classroom with many of the children. Both were excellent teachers and interested in learning to use drama with the children. I did not know the children and they had not done drama before. Although the session went reasonably well, it was certainly "rough" from my perspective as the teacher. In the midst of the drama I even had concerns about my efforts not being a good enough model to convince the teachers to go any farther with drama.

I needn't have worried. Just as I was aware of my concern, I caught a glimpse of the resource teacher hurriedly trying to set up a video camera to capture the improvisations that were developing. A moment later when I wheeled around in role to face one of the groups of children whom I was pressing with a challenge, I also surprisingly faced the principal who had been quickly summoned by the teacher to come see what the children were doing. This unexpected attention was a bit disconcerting, but I finished the session and said my good-byes to the class. It was only in my discussion with the teachers later that morning that I understood the significance of the flurry of activity.

In short, despite their excellent ability as teachers, they were both astonished at the previously unseen creativity, insight, and social skills shown by the children in role. In addition, since it was a French immersion classroom, the children were doing the drama session in their second (or even third) language and the teachers were equally surprised at the quality of the children's French in role. I tell this story *not* to indicate what a wonderful drama teacher I am. If anything, I saw a number of areas I needed to work on and refine as a teacher. Rather, I tell this story to indicate the power of improvised drama as a learning medium for learners. In drama, we are at play in a certain sense and, as Vygotsky (1960) noted so insightfully, the child at play is "a head taller" than himself or herself at other times. In other words, play is a way that the learner extends his or her development through imagination in an interactive and safe context for exploration. While Vygotsky was speaking of young children, I believe the principle probably applies for all learners, regardless of age. The reactions of the teachers of the grade 5 class I worked with certainly seem to support Vygotsky's comment. What convinced them of the power of drama was not my efforts as the leader, but rather the ideas, the language, the interactions of the children that drama tapped into and fostered.

I've taken some time to share this story since I feel that much of the true power of this volume lies in the many examples of what learners have created in various contexts and subject areas. The examples range from eloquent writing, to moving poetry, to deep insight, to creative response, and so on. As I read through the chapters, I am convinced again and again of the power of drama as a learning medium across the curriculum. I am convinced, yes, partly by the various teachers who use the Fictional Family techniques creatively and sensitively, but particularly by the learners who seem to have benefited from the techniques and whose learning is so evident in what they produce.

I invite you now to read these descriptions and to judge for yourself. I hope that the Fictional Family technique might serve as an addition to your existing repertoire of drama methods or perhaps might provide enough structure and support for you to try drama as a learning medium for the first time. In any case, it is the quality and potential of students' learning which this volume places in the spotlight and which drama seeks to serve.

DAVID DILLON

References

Gold, Muriel. *The Fictional Family.* Springfield, IL: Charles C. Thomas Publisher, 1991.

Heathcote, Dorothy. *Three Looms Waiting.* BBC Television production, 1971.

Vygotsky, Lev. *Thought and Language.* Cambridge, MA: MIT Press, 1960.

Preface

In her brilliantly written novel, *Anansi*, quoted in the epigraph to this book, Anne Hébert describes the despair of her protagonist, Pierrette Paul, who is overcome by the thought that she will be confined to being herself, with no possibility for change, for the rest of her life. Pierrette's solution is to become a professional actress.

In working with the Fictional Family, students have an opportunity to create and "inhabit" a character different from themselves, to live in its skin, to experience situations and a family life different from their own, without necessarily committing themselves to acting as a professional career. In my first book, *THE FICTIONAL FAMILY in Drama, Education and Groupwork*, I asked, "What If" you could temporarily belong to a different family, have different parents and siblings, different grandparents, different extended families, and live in an environment different from your own-richer, poorer, rural, urban-or even in a different historical era-how would this experience affect your personality, your attitudes and lifestyle? And, after having experienced your new character in a variety of new situations, how would this ultimately affect your choices in life?

The book described the Fictional Family technique in an introductory university acting class; it demonstrated a step-by-step approach that could be adapted for use in a variety of other disciplines, but *it left it up to individual professionals to adapt it for their own use.* It discussed the relationship of the technique to the Stanislavski System, Brecht's Epic Theatre, Theatre of the Absurd, and to other actor-training techniques.

In my second book, *THERAPY THROUGH DRAMA: THE FICTIONAL FAMILY*, I focused on the *therapeutic applications* of the technique. I described the Fictional Family's use with specific populations (family therapy trainees, drama therapists, graduate drama therapy students, and drama students) and focused on particular themes (rape survival, improvisational scene-work training, and transformative learning). Four of the seven chapters were contributions by other authors who have worked with the technique.

This third book, *DRAMA ACROSS THE CURRICULUM: The Fictional Family in Practice*, evolved after discussions with professors in teacher-education programs who were seeking texts with innovative methodologies to enhance student learning. They stated that such a text would greatly strengthen the under-represented area of drama across the curriculum. They found the metaphor of the Fictional Family pedagogically interesting, and readily applicable across learning/teaching disciplines. They thought that the proposed text could serve an important leadership role in a strong and growing "literacy across the curriculum" movement.

Five of the nine chapters have been written by authors other than myself, who offer examples of how the technique has been used in their particular disciplines to counteract stultifying factual learning, and to encourage creative and critical thinking in an exciting and nurturing environment.

A Note about Repetition

I have wished each chapter to be an entity unto itself, therefore the reader of the entire book may find a few passages repetitious. Also, versions of some chapters were published in my previous publications.

Organization of the Book

This volume explores the use of the Fictional Family methodology to enhance students' learning across the curriculum in secondary and post-secondary programs. **Chapter One** introduces the basic Fictional Family technique as I designed, developed and used it in a university-based drama course. Students create characters from their own imaginations, live with, and enact these characters for an extended period of time within the ensemble of a family unit, and through this process they are able to create credible, multidimensional characters.

University instructors teaching language arts and/or language across the curriculum as well as teachers across the curriculum who are not drama teachers need not be intimidated by the Fictional Family methodology. They need not feel that they must be trained in drama to apply the methodology to their various disciplines. First, unlike other drama methodologies (Heathcote, Bolton, O'Neill), the teacher is not "in role" as a teaching strategy. Often teachers who are not drama specialists find the prospect of working in role daunting.

Second, the technique, with its familiar structure, quickly engages students in writing and improvising. And the inherent goals of the methodology-to enhance personal growth, to nurture, to stimulate, to validate their efforts-are all compatible goals of the teacher in any subject area. It is the students' efforts and involvement and excitement which will ultimately be key to their successful learning.

The chapter provides a *goal-oriented step-by-step approach* which educators can follow and/or adapt according to the specific learning goals of their particular disciplines.

Chapter Two provides a general rationale for drama as a learning medium by exposing its link with a *Language Across the Curriculum* approach to teaching. The application of the Fictional Family methodology as a learning medium in classrooms is explored. Dr. Dillon offers examples of a number of possible Fictional Family scenarios from various subject areas—language arts, social studies, moral and religious education, *etc.*—which can complement and enhance the more usual learning means of talk, reading, and writing. He stresses that the goal of organizing students' learning dramatically through the Fictional Family technique does far more than merely providing an interesting alternative to traditional classroom work. Rather, it can powerfully shape the very way in which learners come to understand the information they encounter in school.

Few teachers have had experience with drama as a learning medium, particularly its approach of evoking from students rather than directing them. Most teachers need a structure or protocol within which to begin using drama for learning. The Fictional Family methodology offers such structure for teachers while still leaving some openness within it for improvisational and creative possibilities.

In **Chapter Three**, Judy Kalman demonstrates the use of the Fictional Family methodology in the context of a particular university composition course and discusses how the technique was implemented to teach effective Writing Across the Curriculum (WAC).

After searching for new ways to make writing exciting for her students and to bridge the gap between writing and knowledge in other areas, Kalman was drawn to the idea of the Fictional Family construct. She began to spin exciting scenarios of how she could use this method to teach rhetorical modes to her students, how it would lend itself to descriptive, narrative and even persuasive writing, and how students could stretch their abilities within the security of a self-created, nurturing environment.

The author describes how the technique lends itself to three categories of writing: transactional, expressive, and poetic. The chapter refers to the philosophies of WAC and educational theorists such as James Britton, Bryant Fillion, Mary Barr, Mary Healy, David Russell and Toby Fulwiler.

Looking at the technique from a purely pedagogic viewpoint, she had no idea what excitement Fictional Family would engender in students from all disciplines, from fine arts to business, an excitement which remained a satisfaction to encounter. Students in her classes offer analyses of what makes learning and language happen in her classes.

Chapter Four illustrates the technique's use in the development of writing skills-in creative writing (playwriting, narrative, poetry)-journals, free-flow inner monologues and integration of individual work to create performance pieces. I offer examples of my students' writing inspired by the stimuli of the Fictional Family's use of visualization, physicalization and improvisational exercises.

Inventing biographical scenarios to develop character is valuable not only for actors but also for writers of fiction such as novelists, playwrights and screenwriters. The moment a character is born, its interior life begins. As the story unfolds, the exterior life of the character develops. The interaction between the character and its environment, the obstacles it encounters, and its behaviour and responses to that environment and those obstacles, reveal the character's personality.

In **Chapter Five** Michael Sommers describes his experience of linking poetry writing and acting while participating in my drama class. He notes the similarities between the two disciplines-both require imagination, experimentation, and rigorous attention to precise detail. Both are imitations of life, attempting to create more vivid, colourfully-interpreted landscapes. Both give creative expression to themes, issues, conflicts, and situations that occur in the world. And both offer their own solutions to them. Both disciplines also strive to entertain, to stir, and to move their audiences by taking into account all of the human senses and their reactions.

Given the freedom to let his imagination run wild, Sommers' journal writing became richer as it reflected the acting activities and exercises experienced in the classes. Offering many examples of the writing inspired by the activities which he experienced as his character, Snake Jordan, in his fictional family, he critiques his own writing pointing out, for example, his use of active verbs reflecting mood, creating rhythm and speed to create dynamic writing. He concludes by saying that an environment which nurtures creativity and freedom-acting, through its many facets-can inspire poetry.

Student needs in the new millennium are forcing the adoption of new academic standards, which are in turn producing the need for new approaches to the teaching of history in the classroom. In **Chapter Six** Samuel Kalman proposes that teachers must cease to view the classroom as solely textbook and lecture-based, using rote memorization and exams as the only classroom tools of any practical use. Studies have shown again and again that most students do not retain information in such an environment.

The author refers to Howard Gardner and his work on Multiple Intelligence Theory, which has demonstrated that some students are visual, some are auditory, and some learn more through written exercises. Thus their ability to think critically or to perform certain tasks cannot be adequately gauged through note-taking. Dr. Kalman asks how we can therefore move away from this exclusive methodology.

The Fictional Family model combines auditory, written, and visual learning while at the same time provoking students to think critically, rather than merely repeating facts handed out in a textbook or a lecture. The emphasis in this exercise is on a real understanding of history, and its inherent complexity, which the text or lecture often cannot convey.

Dr. Kalman offers possible scenarios which fit the era being studied, such as the French Revolution, in which fictional families respectively represent the peasantry, the emerging bourgeoisie, the nobility, and church (perhaps a group of priests from the same abbey); the era of Imperialism, and the Napoleonic era. By adopting a point of view, a distinctive perspective on the events of the day, rather than merely reading about the various doctrinal positions in a textbook; students must become the characters about which they read, mobilizing the wealth of textbook and lecture material amassed in prior weeks, to create an authentic historical agent.

Chapter Seven offers a guide to how the technique can be used as a learning medium in the classroom in the teaching of literature. It has long been the preserve of the English teacher to help students learn to experience literature, or stories, more fully and deeply, particularly through understanding and identifying with various characters. This step can be difficult when characters in a story represent life experience quite different from those of the students who encounter them. Yet the success or failure of students in "seeing through the eyes" of a character is a key factor affecting the quality of their experience of a story.

In recent years, new expectations have also cut across the curriculum, affecting all teachers regardless of their traditional subject matter expertise. One such new expectation is multicultural education, designed to help us all understand and at least tolerate, if not appreciate, the cultural and social differences among the North American population, differences which increasingly exist in close contact with each other in our cities and our classrooms. Another goal of multicultural education is to combat ignorance of others who are different from us, thus freeing us from fear of each other.

I propose that these two goals of literature teaching and multicultural education can be integrated and achieved together. The Fictional Family methodology has the potential to offer students the experience of relating to a diversity of cultures at the same time as they explore the understanding of and identification with fictional characters.

While this chapter deals specifically with diversity and multiculturalism, a wide variety of social issues appear in the scenarios of the fictional families, such as ageism, sexual assault, mental and physical disabilities, death, divorce, substance abuse, bullying, stepfamilies and teen-age suicide. These topics should be inseparable from the work with Fictional Family.

Despite widespread acknowledgement of the importance of dealing with gender issues in education, their treatment in schooling still remains a problematic area. In the domain of theatre arts, there is a lack of material connecting gender and acting pedagogy, **Chapter Eight** concludes that gender in the drama class is not sufficiently addressed. Similarly, books focused on gender issues in family dynamics are not very common. There is a lack of appreciation for gender differences in both disciplines.

The Fictional Family technique can work as a powerful tool to create awareness in its participants of gender discrimination, sexual stereotyping, and traditional perspectives of women as lesser contributors to a variety of cultures and fields. Through dramatic enactment of their fictional family characters' lives, societal attitudes and behaviours are clearly reflected, giving teachers an ideal opportunity to underline the connections between these attitudes and behaviours. By seizing this opportunity, they can facilitate the group's sensitivity to, and awareness of, the possibility of effecting change.

Numerous examples from the scenarios enacted in classes are offered which range from such topics as lesbianism, family violence, eating disorders and other more subtle manifestations of sex differentiation. A student argued in her paper that "the fictional family technique has a stronger impact than feminist theatre because of its use of interesting poly-dimensional characters as opposed to the flat stereotype characters often found in feminist theatre".

The Fictional Family technique can address gender issues through scripted plays. An approach to Ibsen's *A Doll's House* is described in detail.

Chapter Nine explores in some detail the process of planning for the use of the Fictional Family technique as part of one's own subject matter.

Dr. Dillon gives specific examples of how the scenarios can be used to teach not only such subjects as English literature, composition, creative writing, and history as described in earlier chapters, but also principles of ecology in the Science and Technology field, and economics in the Social Studies field.

Drama always deals in very specific and particular examples. Thus, basing drama activities on ecological issues usually means looking at very specific and localized examples of these larger issues. That is, the causes and effects of one family's activity on the planet's ecology, as well as local social issues on environmental concerns. He outlines the preliminary steps, the character and context development, conflict over environmental issues in the fictional family groups, and several other scenarios that are inherent in the Fictional Family technique which enlighten students to the applicability of ecological principles and their responsibilities around them- both within the family and the home- to a broader social arena.

In applying the Fictional Family technique (step-by-step) to economics education, and to some extent geography, Dr. Dillon encourages students to explore the interrelated aspects and the cause-and-effect dynamics of the various components of an economic system. They infer and imagine the future implications of today's current economic situation for families in various parts of our global economic system.

MURIEL GOLD

Acknowledgements

I wish to express my gratitude:

To David Dillon who read the manuscript throughout its development offering valuable suggestions.

To the contributors to the volume: David Dillon, Judy Kalman, Michael Sommers, and Samuel Kalman

To Robert Landy whose technique, "Extended Dramatization" with graduate drama therapy students inspired me to initiate my "Fictional Family" methodology.

To the talented Cecilia Ugarte for her creative cartoons.

To my husband, Dr. Ronald Poole, for scanning the illustrations and formatting and proof-reading the manuscript.

Contents

Chapter One:

The Fictional Family in the Drama Class

Muriel Gold

The Fictional Family (FF) technique was initiated, researched and developed in my drama classes over a period of several years. While this volume explores the use of the FF technique to enhance students' learning across the curriculum in secondary and post-secondary programs, the purpose of this chapter is to describe the basic technique as I developed and used it in a university-level drama course.

However, the technique can also be used in a number of other settings for various purposes. To date I have used the FF technique with Drama in Education students, with students in advanced acting classes, and with actors in the rehearsal process. I have also used it in other settings with varying goals and time frames. Some of my former students, now teachers, have used the methodology with their own High School students both in their drama classes and in other subject areas. They have found it to be a powerful springboard to engage students in dramatic activity and to inspire learning.

For ten years (1986-96) I used the technique at McGill University in an undergraduate university course designed to explore the actor's resources-voice, body, senses, imagination, intellect-as an aid to personal growth and an understanding of the acting process. The course took the view of Hodgson and Richards (1966) that "the qualities needed for the best acting are also those qualities required for the fullest living".

The Learning Potential

In the FF structure, the class is subdivided into groups of five students. Each group invents a fictional family and the members of this group give their family a name, historical background, geographical location, and identify the various family members' ages and positions within the family. Students then develop their own fictional family characters by defining the character's birthplace, personal history, profession, income, religion, likes and dislikes, personal relationships to, and attitudes towards, the other family members.

Throughout the course students create and perform a sequence of scenes, each designed to achieve particular character-development objectives. These objectives include building concentration skills, vocal and physical expression, communication ability, trust, and character believability. All scenes contain objectives intended to externalize and develop the relationships (initially created on paper) between fictional family members.

To give fictional families a feeling of experienced reality, students perform past events in their fictional family characters' lives; to help them envision new sets of possibilities for their characters, they perform scenes that might take place in the future.

All scenes are preceded by visualization and physicalization techniques to assist actors in their character-development process. Visualization techniques involve stimulating actors through sense memory to recall or create mental images. Whereas these visualization exercises are aimed to assist actors to develop their characters' emotional lives, physicalization techniques are aimed to create characters' physical lives. Since voice and body are an integral unit, physicalization techniques include freeing vocal expression.

The beginning work is based on the Stanislavski System of naturalistic acting. Emphasis is placed on developing the inner psychological approach to character creation. In reaction to overacting, clichés and mannerisms, Stanislavski, the great Russian director, developed a methodology to help actors develop and portray truthful and believable characters (Moore, 1987).

Why choose to work within a Fictional Family framework?

The family forms a common basis of experience, a unit to which everyone can relate. Even the most sheltered and naive university and high school students have been exposed all their lives to the depth and intricacy of family relationships of one sort or another. Their perceptions, their communication styles and their modes of interacting have been shaped initially and significantly within the processes of their own family dynamics.

The FF structure provides the actors with an opportunity to choose a position or age status in the fictional family similar or dissimilar to their position in their real-life families. They can choose to replay experienced family conflicts and sibling rivalry, or invent new or previously imagined family situations and controversies. They can play out their fantasy character. For example, had they always wished to be the independent older child, or the spoiled baby, they can now delve into this character and discover the advantages and disadvantages each person encounters whatever his or her position in the family, and in life, may be.

Enacting dramatic situations within their fictional families over an extended period of time allows actors to expand their knowledge and intuitive understanding of the varied backgrounds and communication styles of others. It can increase their sensitivity and compassion, and develop their awareness of the psychological profile, of both of their own fictional family character and the fictional family characters with whom they interact.

The further students delve into their fictional family characters, the more they discover about that character, about themselves, and about their fictional and real environment. This analysis and self-discovery can enrich both their potential as actors and as human beings. A student who had participated in the FF experience subsequently wrote:

> I have learned a lot from playing Nick. I have learned how infuriating it can be for people who love somebody to deal with them when they are so smug and sarcastic. I, to some extent, am like Nick…my outlook used to be very similar to Nick's. Similarly to what my [fictional] family is telling Nick, my own family told me that my attitude was both tiring and irritating to cope with 24 hours a day…I suppose I did not feel very good about myself. I learned how difficult sarcastic people are, and how much value there is in listening to people.

Within the FF framework, student actors can work on many aspects of theatre training. This training includes skills particular to the theatre such as building a character, designing stage picturization and blocking, and identifying performance style; as well as skills with wider application such as personal development, creative writing, and teamwork.

Because students conceive and create their roles from their imagination and observations, and develop scenes in collaboration with their fictional family group, they acquire an understanding of the steps involved in developing characterization. They can now apply this technique to a role conceived and written by a playwright. In addition, they have been part of a collective creation; this experience will be valuable background for future theatre ensemble work.

Sarcastic Nick

Theatre practitioners recognize that beginning actors generally lack self-confidence, are reluctant to take initiative, and are apprehensive of peer response. They seek constant approval and support. The FF offers to these student actors a built-in support group, where they can progress at their own speed, benefit from the creative input and energy of their family members, and gain the security which arises from group solidarity.

One of my students eloquently expressed this experience in her mid-term essay.

> Angela Forbes was created on an empty canvas. The few wooden planks, the framework surrounding the canvas, offered the only boundaries of creativity. With every stroke of the artist's brush, her figure took shape. At first her form was awkward and lacked definition. Mistakes were made and then covered up, or they were merely altered to a correct form. The artist had her intellect to guide her, as well as her intuition.

5

The process was long and often difficult, causing frustration, yet in the pursuit of knowledge, many unexpected discoveries were made that added to the creative effort. The confidence of one day far outlasted the disappointment of others, and offered a challenge to do better the next time.

In the end, the painting became part of the artist and could not have existed without her. In return, the artist grew through her attempts to create art.

The FF unit and the fictional characters it contains will develop, grow and change over an extended period responding to the needs, perceptions, and discoveries of the fictional family members.

Methods and Time Scale

This chapter describes the use of the FF technique in a thirteen-week introductory university drama class. However I have used the technique in a variety of shorter time frames with a variety of student classes. For example, I have used it at McGill with graduate social work students in a time frame of six two-hour weekly sessions. And I have been working within the same time frame for the past four years with graduate Drama Therapy students at Concordia University.

When I was first invited to work within the shorter time span, I was concerned that this length of time would not allow students adequate time to delve into their characters. To my surprise, the students reported that they became very absorbed with their characters and that throughout the week, they were thinking of creative ways to develop them into multidimensional beings. The character diaries they wrote were instrumental in sustaining their interest. By the end of the six-week period they reported (in an evaluation sheet) that they had learned a great deal about their characters, gained insight about themselves, and had been exposed to a brief introduction of acting techniques.

Angela Forbes Canvas

I have also used FF with high school drama teachers in one-day workshops to enhance their repertoire of dramatic techniques. To my surprise, there was a vast discrepancy in drama background within this group. Some drama teachers (the minority) had twenty years background in the teaching of drama, some had very limited experience and some admitted that they were parachuted by the principal into teaching a subject in which they had no experience and worse, no previous interest. The first group, at first, looked sceptical, but as the workshop proceeded became enthusiastic. The second group was eager to augment their limited knowledge and the last group, needless to say, was desperate to learn some kind of technique.

At Dawson, a Junior College, I incorporated the technique into a fifteen-week Contemporary Theatre class. Again, this time frame worked well. Interspersed with reading of scripts by well-known playwrights, they were inspired to write their own scripts based on their fictional families. Again, I have used the technique over six-session rehearsal periods culminating in a collective creation. The collective creations have resulted in innovative and well-crafted performances. Collective creations refer to the re-enactment of scenes already presented in class which are then organized, polished, rehearsed and performed for an audience.

In the thirteen-week format, before initiating the FF improvisation, a variety of warm-ups are introduced to develop concentration skills, sense awareness, physical relaxation and to stimulate the imagination (see Gold, 1991). Students need to become comfortable with themselves, with group members and with the physical space. The importance of a supportive, nurturing environment within which they can create cannot be overstressed. Guided whole-group improvisations progress to improvisations in pairs or small groups. To allow a variety of group dynamic experiences, students are encouraged to change partners and group members frequently.

Some improvisations involve creative writing, such as the composition of original poems by individual students, then the integration of these poems on paper in pairs or groups for performance (*see Gold, Chapter Four, and Sommers, Chapter Five.*) Some improvisations involve the creation and performance of a fictional character's life by groups of eight or nine students. This improvisation is preceded by guided whole-group improvisations in which students are born, act as infants, then children, progress through the various stages of their lives, become old and/or die. Other small-group improvisations include activities such as statues, puppets, animals, mannequins and machines, and the bringing to life of inanimate objects.

In the university model described here, the FF improvisation is not introduced until the sixth session and, throughout its use, creative warm-ups and improvisations are maintained. During these warm-ups and relaxation exercises students are fed visual, tactual and sound images to help foster their imaginations and lead into the family improvisations *(see below)*.

Suggested Reading

A variety of preparatory exercises can be found in such books as those listed below. The exercises can be used as described, or they may be extended, or adapted to suit your particular group's needs.

Benedetti, Robert: *The Actor at Work*, New Jersey. Prentice Hall, 1970.

Booth, David and Charles Lundy: *Improvisation: Learning Through Drama*. Toronto. Harcourt, Brace Jovanovitch, Canada, Inc., 1985.

Hodgson, John and Ernest Richards. *Improvisation.* London. Methuen and Co.,1966

Moore, Sonia: *Training an Actor.* New York. Penguin, 1985;

Spolin, Viola: *Improvisation for the Theatre.* Evanston. Northwestern University, 1960.

Way, Brian: *Development through Drama.* London. Longman, 1967.

Improvisations

There are five basic FF performance contexts.

a. 'Spontaneous' Improvisations in which students are given little or no time to prepare presentations; my goal here is to assist actors to let their characters speak without preparation so that unexpected characters' emotions and/or thoughts might spontaneously emerge;

b. 'Prepared' Improvisations for which they are given ten or more minutes to prepare and rehearse; here the goal is to foster team collaboration in a limited time frame;

c. 'Polished' Improvisations which they prepare and rehearse out of class, but there is no written script or outline; the objective of these types of improvisations is to allow students to obtain additional input about their character development from their peers;

d. Scenes which are developed out of class from students' original script outlines; this work is designed to start them on collaborative writing, a component considered to be a valid element in the actor's process (Field, 1982);

e. Script development; in addition to developing writing skills, this experience provides students with an additional method of analyzing their characters. They put words into their characters' mouths and then are forced to deliver these particular lines.

Journals

During the thirteen weeks, students write journals describing all class activities and improvisations and expressing their personal reflections. This journal becomes a record of their creative process-the gradual discovery of their inner resources, their needs and inhibitions and their experiential development in the process of character-creation. This information will become useful reference material for them in future work.

The journal also serves as a vehicle for mutual feedback. In a class of twenty-five students working in the allotted time slot, there is little time for extended discussion. Furthermore, students who find themselves inhibited in group exchange are surprisingly articulate, insightful and candid in their journals.

The feedback helps me to assess individual student responses to the class work and to get to know the student more quickly. It also gives me an opportunity to give individual feedback in a private, personal way.

To encourage free expression of thoughts and emotions the writing in the journals is never corrected; comments, supportive in style, pertain to the students' developmental process and their progress.

The Scheme of Work

Step 1. Organization of Fictional Families

The class is arbitrarily divided into groups of five members. Each group is asked to formulate and begin to construct a fictional family. Students are asked to describe in writing, for next class, their fictional family characters with a name, age, personal history, birthplace, profession, income, religion and political viewpoint, as well as a personal relationship with the people in their family. The writing should describe, in the first person, their character's past and present and express its hopes for the future. It should include their character's secret which they withhold from the other fictional family members for use in a later scenario (see Gold, 1991). They also construct fictional family trees going back two generations. They are asked to select a particular object which carries special meaning to their character and to have this object in their possession whenever they assume their role.

Step 2. Scene One. The Fictional Family at Breakfast

The fictional families reinforce their relationships created on paper and present an expository breakfast scene which introduces the family to the larger group. A student wrote in her journal:

> Everyone seemed to fit into their characters so well,
> perhaps because many of us have incorporated facets of
> ourselves or people we know well into our personalities,
> exploiting and exaggerating our own individualities. I
> saw a quietness that was typically Julie, an explosive
> non-conformity in Gary, and in me, maybe a vestige

of bossiness I no doubt inherited from my maternal grandmother, since much of "Granny" was patterned after her. She lived with my family for intermittent periods of years, until my own mother's death.

Step 3. Monologue

Following the breakfast scene, the actors stay in character and each in turn delivers a monologue introducing h/er character. After each monologue, the audience asks the character for clarification or additional information. The monologue and audience participation reinforce the characters which the actors created on paper. They learn from the audience's reactions and questions whether their characters were believable on stage, which characteristics were well-defined and which need further definition. In other words, they discover whether the relationships which they built in theory project across the footlights.

Step 4. Scene Two. The Fictional Family in Conflict

The fictional families present a scene with a conflict. To prepare them for this scene I ask them to decide what it is their character *wants* from a particular family member. Then I ask them to articulate that *want* so that it is very clear in their minds before they start the scene. Sometimes I incorporate a physical mime game (tug of war, squash) as a warm up in which students are forced to focus on winning.

Following the scene the actors remain on stage in character and each in turn answers three basic questions-What do I want? Who or what obstacle is in my path? What do I do to get what I want? It is pointed out that there are many ways to get what one wants. It need not always be through arguing, fighting, or threatening. It can be, for example, through coaxing, manipulating, and/or cajoling. Actors discover that obstacles and the strivings of characters against each other's *wants* or 'objectives' generate more powerful dramatic situations and theatrical scenes (Stanislavski, 1961).

In place of words like objective or motivation, one can use other terminology. Shurtleff (1978) asks his actors, "What are you fighting *for?*" He says the word *fight* inspires actors to find strong goals which in turn create more dynamic scenes.

What are you fighting for?

Identifying *wants* can eventually help to improve communication between fictional family members. When individual fictional family characters come to understand what, specifically they want for themselves and for their fictional families, change can occur within the family dynamic. This awareness can lead toward deeper understanding not only of their fictional characters but also of their real families in their daily lives.

Bandler, Grinder and Satir (1976) apply similar techniques to family therapy. According to these authors, family therapists should continually assist clients to 'identify their wants' in an effort to initiate effective communication between family members.

Step 5. Scene Three The Fictional Family Faces a Crisis
The families perform a holiday dinner scene in which everything goes wrong. (For example, if the improvisation precedes the Canadian Thanksgiving weekend, we would focus on that particular holiday.)

In a preliminary sense-memory exercise it is suggested that students visualize their experiences of Thanksgiving in the past with their actual families-the smells, tastes, sounds, general environment-and then think about their fictional family members and their hopes for a warm, pleasant Thanksgiving dinner. They then congregate in their family groups to develop the Thanksgiving dinner "disaster" for performance. Because each fictional family member wants something different from this event, this improvisation heightens the concept of conflicting objectives between the family members, and builds dramatic tension.

Step 6. Inner Monologues

After the performance, the actors, staying in character, remain seated at their Thanksgiving table and each in turn presents an **inner monologue** addressed separately to one or more of the family without looking at them. These monologues not only continue monologue performance work introduced in the preparatory exercises (*see Chapter Four*) and in Step 3 of the FF process, but also they require actors to probe more deeply their emotions, needs and wants. In articulating their thoughts and inner feelings, they expand their communication style and add further dimensions to the interfamilial relationships.

Addressing family members without looking at them aids concentration; deeper concentration helps actors to focus on their emotions. The family members who are addressed gain insight into that character's psyche as well as their own and this combined insight encourages deeper and more meaningful future group interaction. In fact, all fictional family members gain fresh perceptions from each monologue. Since the actors use their own experiential resources to develop their characters, the discoveries here are important to both character and actor. A student wrote:

> There was no physical movement, or outward action, but the energy inside was very intense. The words flowed rhythmically, emanating almost from the subconscious.

Chapter Four contains some examples of students' inner monologues.

Step 7. Scene Four. Re-enactment

The family re-enacts the scene so that it will end on a positive note. In this replay, the situation remains the same; it is the attitudes of the characters to one another which must change. This should come about as a result of the insight acquired from listening to each other's monologues. This experience helps the student understand the extreme importance of attitude both as an actor on stage and as an individual coping with real-life situations. For example, one student who was playing a young girl whose mother had died asked me how she could possibly end the scene positively without bringing her fictional mother back to life. When I suggested she leave her mother in the grave but change her character's *attitude* to the loss of her mother, she brightened up and re-enacted the scene.

This time she changed her character's objective: from "I want my mother back" to "I'm going to help my family make this dinner a joyous occasion". Playing a "happy" scene also reveals to actors the difficulty of making scenes where conflicts are quickly resolved as interesting and dynamic as unresolved conflict scenes.

Step 8. Fictional Family Houses

Each family designs and sketches a picture of its house, including floor-plans of each room in the house, in order to further establish their characters, solidify their relationships and understand their families' economic and social situations. This exercise necessitates further search into each character's visual, tactile and visceral needs and tastes. A student's journal entry reads:

> We all had such a fantastic time creating our home. The strange part about it, however, was that we kept appearing in character as we threw out ideas. When we gave Julie a small, sandwiched room with no balcony, her character

came right out. "I don't want a small room! Why do
Angela and Doug get the rooms with the balconies?"

The class sits in a circle on the floor and one family member shows
each family's pictures and drawings and describes its house. By now it
becomes evident that the actors feel the families have become real. They
have built a house together. They have agonized over their collective
and individual needs and wants, and have adapted those needs and
wants to the socio-economic reality of the family situation. They have
established, in spite of whatever familial conflicts exist "at home", a
feeling of outward family solidarity. This family reality projects itself
to the group. A student wrote:

> When it came time to describe our mansion to the class,
> it was as if people actually resented us because we were
> rich. One family said, "Well, at least we work for our
> money." Father answered sarcastically, "And I don't?"

Step 9. Scene Five. The Fictional Families Ten Years From Now
During the creative warm-up the students imagine their lives ten years
from now and contemplate their hopes and dreams for the future. Next
they imagine their fictional family characters ten years hence and their
hopes. They bring these to life in their improvised family scenes.

Imagining and enacting situations in their future lives promotes
further levels of understanding of themselves, their characters and the
intricate, real and fictional family relationships. This understanding can
lead to the envisaging of a whole new set of possibilities and ideas for
overcoming obstacles which will encourage change within the situation.
The development of an unrestrained imagination, in other words, the
ability to fantasize, will motivate actors to break new ground artistically
and to be innovative and creative in their theatre work.

Step 10. Scene Six. The Fictional Family Ten Years Ago

There can be no present without a past. To improvise a sequence from the family's life ten years prior lifts the character from the printed page, makes history an experienced reality, and elucidates the present situation. Again this improvisation is preceded by creative warm-ups. A student wrote:

> I gained more insight about our family by reflecting on our past. Ten years ago we were more of a 'family' than we are now. Christmas eves were always enjoyable for the Normal family. I was shocked to find out Santa Claus didn't exist, but I soon realized that the 'spirit of Christmas' lives on. I admired Steven back then. After all he was my 'big brother' and could do no wrong. Mother has done a good job of bringing the family up without Dad's support. I think the Christmas when I was seven was the best ever. *Joyeux Noel*, everyone!

Step 11. From Stanislavski to Bertolt Brecht

Work with students on performance style begins. I select Brecht at this point for the following reasons:

1. Having exposed the students to Stanislavski's naturalistic style where character-identification is all important, it now seems a good idea to introduce them to Brecht's alienation techniques where the actors must learn to distance themselves from their roles, to separate the character from the self. In other words, instead of attempting to get into the "skin" of their characters, they now become actors playing a role, and this helps students to discover additional dimensions of their characters.

The actor's goal is to reach the rational, analytic part of spectators, so that, instead of being swept away by the emotional aspect of the drama, the audience will relate to the play's social message. Brecht believed that society could change and that theatre was a powerful medium to effect that change.

2. Because Brecht's theatre involves character gestus, *i.e.*, precise physical representation of the character's attitude and point of view, it is an effective style to introduce the concept of physical embodiment of a role.

3. Since many of the fictional families present conflicts which are potential social issues, Brecht's theme-centred style, his emphasis on social and political realities and his didactic approach facilitates thought and reflection about the problems presented in the families in particular and with social issues in general.

4. Other important components of Brechtian theatre such as scenic gestus, spatial environment which reinforces the action of the play; simple, selective and functional costumes and properties; masks to indicate character attitude, all offer students an opportunity to create and utilize masks and symbolic props. The spatial, episodic structure of Brecht's style produces an awareness of how to utilize space in more innovative ways. Music and song, which Brecht incorporated in his plays to further his alienation technique, *i.e.*, to interrupt the story, allows music students in the class to contribute an added quality to the scenes.

Step 12. Exercises, Improvisations, and Games

The next three sessions are devoted to the kinds of exercises, games and improvisations suggested by theatre directors such as John Harrop and Sabin Epstein. Professor Harrop heads the acting program at University of California at Santa Barbara, and Sabin Epstein is based in New York City where he has been associate director of such prestigious companies as La Mama and the American Conservatory Theatre in San Francisco. Their book, *Acting with Style*, (1982) offers a series of over 100 games and exercises to help the actor approach a variety of performance styles. There is a section on Brecht and what Brecht calls 'epic acting'. The exercises help students to develop physical characterization and create character 'gestus'.

Brecht and the Fictional Family Characters

Having developed the fictional family characters using Stanislavski's inner technique -playing the personal, emotional response of the character to a particular situation, the students are now exposed to Brecht's ideas of "truthful" performances-where the actors are themselves, and present characters upon whom they pass comment, and where emotion must be communicated through a recognizable action. The warm-ups centre on physical activity which explores the moving rhythms and energies of a variety of characters with specific socio-economic functions in a modern political structure. Improvisations revolve around situations featuring socio-economic themes.

Example 1. Character Types

Move around in the space. Focus on your breathing, and on your body rhythm. With what part of your body do you lead? Some people lead with their head; others with their knees, their hips, and so. Exaggerate. When I clap my hands, freeze. I will call out a particular character type. Form an image of that character. Feel your body transforming into that character. Then move as that character.

First character type: Teacher. Freeze in an attitude which represents the image of a teacher. Exaggerate the attitude. Move as that teacher. Perform that teacher's principal daily activity-the teacher's function in society.

Repeat the exercise as: Soldiers, Lawyers, Doctors, Labor Unionists, Diplomats, Judges, Mayors, Politicians, Police Officers, Firefighters.

Example 2. Social Issue

Having introduced the idea of character types and their functions in society, the class is now divided into groups and asked to create an improvisation focused on a socioeconomic theme. Examples: police brutality, domestic violence, abortion, poverty, capital punishment.

(For further examples of improvisations and students' responses, see Gold, 1991).

Step 13. Scene Seven. Fictional Family Scene (Brechtian Style)

In creating Brechtian fictional family scenes, each family, having selected a socioeconomic theme appropriate for its family, meets between sessions to develop, write and rehearse its scenes.

The presentations are Brechtian in style and flavor. Alienation techniques-masks, signs, symbols, chalkboard slogans, ballads, limericks, narrators- are used. A student wrote:

> Studying Brecht and figuring out how to play my character within the limits of his style really helped me to get a clear notion of the key points of my personality. I felt I was acting as my character instead of as Becky thinking what would Laura be saying, thinking, doing now?

Step 14. Fictional Family Sculptures

A. Each fictional family forms a sculpture which demonstrates the family relationships and the position of each member within the family unit. The audience observes the formation of this sculpture and studies its final presentation. During evaluation, the audience members are asked whether they think the sculpture truly represents the family dynamic. Suggestions are made, and rearrangements take place until both actors and audience are comfortable with the product.

I borrowed this technique from socio-drama where it is used as a group-learning procedure to provide practice in solving human-relations problems and to heighten awareness of real-life family relationships. In the FF approach it serves the same purpose by enhancing awareness of the characters' often unexpressed and/or subconscious feelings towards one another. This awareness promotes articulation of these emotions and communication:

> It is very interesting to watch and give ideas, as well as being re-arranged. I look forward to more opportunities to hear how others experience my character, how he is coming across. Our family has grown very close, oddly enough!, as if we've been together for ages.

B. At other times I might ask the fictional families to create a *series* of sculptures: each fictional family member is asked to create two sculptures, the first representing the family dynamic as seen by him or her in the present 'actual', the second representing his or her vision of the 'ideal' dynamic. This exercise promotes insight into the particular psyche of each fictional family character. Biases are revealed as well as perceptions and mis-perceptions of interrelationships, facilitating further exploration of the family dynamic.

C. The families once again form sculptures-this time the formation symbolizes a socioeconomic theme relevant to their particular family. For example, the wealthy Forbes family presented themselves in the form of a money tree.

The sculpture technique provides a good opportunity to teach static sense-the position of the actor's body in space, its balance and body position. It gives actors a chance to explore poses the character might assume when walking, talking or listening in a given state of mind. It teaches grouping and blocking-all are necessary skills for visual presentation.

Step 15. Fictional Family Cloning

The groups are exposed to warm-ups and games which involve adopting the gestus of other characters as portrayed in their Brechtian family scenes, and subsequently guessing which character's gestus is being presented. The group sits in a circle and the players in turn present their "clone" to the group by performing a simple action. The group has to identify the family character being cloned. This game reinforces the concept of character gestus; it also serves as an exercise in movement recall, body awareness and communication of the character's physical qualities and expressions.

An unexpected aspect of this exercise was expressed by students in their journals. One student wrote:

When my character (Naomi) was being imitated by Isabelle, I was the last to recognize it. The bizarre fact of the matter is that the other class members almost immediately guessed…I suppose that it may be concluded that we rarely see ourselves the way others do.

Step 16. Establishing Relationships between FFs

At my suggestion that some fictional family members might know each other or have known each other in the past, the families now join together in groups of two or three families to establish relationships which could link them together for a future encounter. The goal is to have a combined Christmas or holiday party. Scenes are presented which show the relationships between individual members which result in an invitation to the party. Some families relate through the children who knew each other at school; some mothers discover they had attended high school together; some are long lost relatives; one person discovers his biological mother.

This mingling of the families is designed to prepare the students for next term when they will be encouraged to initiate and develop scenes which involve any number of actors and combinations of families in any form of work-monologues, two-character scenes featuring actors from different families-that will continue to promote character development and plot, and will give the actors an opportunity to work with other members of the class. It also forces them to work on organization and timing. With a larger cast of characters they learn that they must listen to what the other characters are saying, observe their movements and co-ordinate their own movements and speeches with the rest of the cast. Heightening the awareness of their environment will result in tighter dialogue and more effective blocking and stage business.

Step 17. Scene Eight. The Party

At the final session of the first term, the fictional families present their party scenes. In the first inter-family presentations, characters are often talking at once and there is some confusion. In the second presentation, the party scene, families have discovered ways to organize and plan their scenes for more cohesive and coherent performance. Here again students discover more about their characters' personalities. For example, the wealthy Forbes family threw a surprise party for their mother, Gloria. The scene began with the Forbes family characters in frozen positions on stage. Then each in turn presented a monologue with accompanying movement, describing how they felt about themselves, the family and the imminent party. After each monologue, they exchanged places with the next performer and resumed a static position.

As each fictional family entered the Forbes' "mansion" the various connections between individual characters, established and presented in the previous session, were maintained. By the time the last two families arrived the mood was jubilant; everyone was talking at once; there was no audience to worry about. I had been ushered into the party at some point and interacted with all the characters. Then Mr. Forbes took over and organized some solo performances which developed into group singing. A student wrote:

It was interesting to see everyone maintaining their characters throughout, and interacting with other characters they hadn't encountered before. What a great way to end the term. The carolling at the end was so beautiful. It was a bit frustrating at first. I thought Heidi would be too shy to sing with such a large group of people. But it turned out that singing was the one thing that brought her out of her shell; she could communicate with others, rather than to others, and she gradually started using her rather rusty voice. She was having a great time.

Second Term

In the second eleven-week term, variations of scenes include interaction with members of other families, role reversals within the family, whole family reversals (one family plays another family), a continuation of performance style, more elaborate presentations with sets and props and video playback for self-analysis. For example, one actor playing a wife and mother divorced her family to become liberated. In a series of self-discovering monologues she turned to the occult, discovered she had talent as a writer, performed telephone conversations with literary agents and eventually led a meditation exercise with the class as participants. Another, playing a fourteen-year-old, ran away from home, her step-sister followed her and together they hitchhiked across the country to find her roots in Vancouver.

Group Dynamics

In any group work situation, there will be those who dominate, those who are reticent to voice their opinions and those who do not adequately contribute to the team. The FF situation contains the potential for combinations of such people. Developing the plot and enacting the fictional family story helps the students overcome these problems. By revealing their characters' feelings and emotions and participating in the family dynamic, they themselves learn to listen to others, respect others' opinions, voice their own thoughts and feelings and become a full-fledged member of the creative team.

It could happen, however, that some student or students may feel 'stuck' in a role or in a fictional family. It is advisable to let them know from the outset that they will be staying with these fictional families and in these roles for some time. They are asked to consider this fact carefully before any definitive choices are made. They are warned that, for example, selecting a "child" role might seem appealing, but are they prepared to play that child's role for an extended period of time? These caveats are aimed to rule out frivolous choices and superficial attitudes to selection both of roles and of family types.

They should also be told that this project will not preclude continuance of other work which does not involve the fictional families, and that they will therefore have the opportunity to play a variety of roles both within the FF structure (playing other characters as needed for particular scenes) in addition to roles from other texts.

Teacher's Role

By the end of the course, students will have experienced their characters in a large variety of situations, locations and relationships, both inside and outside their own fictional families; they will have presented their characters through monologue, dialogue, in small and large group scenes; they have performed scenes initiated by me, suggested by their peers, and created themselves.

It is not surprising, therefore, that the actors ultimately relate strongly to, and identify closely with, their fictional family characters and their fictional families. They share their characters' joys and successes, and feel their characters' defeats and pain.

At the same time, the actors are constantly reminded, through the course's emphasis on acting technique, that their characters are fictional; they can only live, breathe and interact at the actors' will. While a character may contain, in varying degrees, aspects of its creator, it remains an imaginary character created for the purpose of learning in the environment of an acting class.

This 'distancing' from the role is the element which controls the merging of the actor with self, and allows the comfort and freedom to allow *the character* to manifest its personality in a variety of ways, such as venting its anger, displaying its 'worst' features, presenting its subconscious or conscious desires and fears (through inner monologues and dreams), projecting its future life, and opening up events, sometimes painful, in its past life.

In early sessions, it may be necessary to emphasize that the confrontations on stage are between the fictional characters, and not the participants. The actor/individual's actions, therefore, are not in question, except in relation to acting craft. Did the actor 'get across' to the audience the character's wishes, feelings and actions? If not, how could the scene be improved?

University instructors teaching language arts and/or language across the curriculum as well as teachers across the curriculum who are not drama teachers need not be intimidated by the FF methodology. They need not feel that they must be trained in drama to apply the methodology to their various disciplines. First, unlike other drama methodologies (Heathcote, Bolton, O'Neill), the teacher is not "in role" as a teaching strategy. Often teachers who are not drama specialists find the prospect of working in role daunting.

Second, the technique, with its familiar structure, quickly engages students in writing and improvising. And the inherent goals of the methodology-to enhance personal growth, to nurture, to stimulate, to validate their efforts-are all compatible goals of the teacher in any subject area. It is the students' efforts and involvement and excitement which will ultimately be key to their successful learning.

References

Bandler, Richard, John Grinder and Virginia Satir. *Changing With Families.* Palo Alto. Science and Behavior Books Inc., 1976

Bolton, Gavin. *Drama as Education: An Argument for Placing Drama at the Centre of the Curriculum.* London. Longman, 1984.

Brecht, Bertolt. *Brecht on Theatre.* translated by John Willett. New York. Hill and Wang, 1964

Gold, Muriel. *The Fictional Family: In Drama, Education and Groupwork.* Springfield, Ill. Charles C Thomas, 1991.

Gold, Muriel. *Therapy Through Drama: The Fictional Family.* Springfield, Ill. Charles C Thomas, 2000

Harrop, John and Sabin Epstein. *Acting with Style..* Prentice-Hall. Englewood Cliffs, New Jersey, 1982.

Heathcote, Dorothy and Gavin Bolton. *Drama for Learning.* Portsmouth, NH. Heinemann, 1995.

Hodgson, John and Ernest Richards. *Improvisation.* London. Methuen and Company, 1969.

Moore, Sonia. *The Stanislavski System.* New York. Penguin Books, 1987

O'Neill, Cecily. *Process Drama.* Portsmouth, NH. Heinemann, 1995.

Shurtleff, Michael. *Audition.* New York. Walker & Co., 1978.

Stanislavski, Constantin. *Creating a Role.* translated by Elisabeth Hapgood. New York. Theatre Arts, 1961.

Chapter Two:

The Fictional Family at Work Across the Curriculum

David Dillon

Romeo reveals his secret to his parents, namely, that he loves Juliet and wishes to marry her. In the light of this disclosure, he faces his parents' wrath, but tries to understand their resistance and to convince them to help him somehow.

The daughter in a family becomes pregnant and considers abortion. Various members of the family have different answers about what is "the right thing to do." The tension is played out to a decision. The next scene is the same family ten years later, in light of whatever the original decision was.

The year is 1933. The Great Depression has settled over the country. Various families from different social classes, races, occupations, and regions of the country face the tensions among themselves caused by the effects of the Depression.

A young, idealistic son launches a crusade at home to have his family live their daily lives in a more ecologically friendly and responsible way. As his middle-class family explores exactly what is implied by this principle, members of the family have various reactions to his proposals for a changed lifestyle.

All these scenarios offer the possibility of students learning across the curriculum-language arts, moral and religious education, social studies, science-by improvising the dynamics of particular fictional families in various times, places, and circumstances. The goal of organizing students' learning dramatically through the Fictional Family (FF) technique is far more than providing an interesting alternative to traditional classroom work, Rather, it can powerfully shape the very way in which learners come to understand the information they encounter in school.

There is widespread agreement on the benefits of improvisational drama as a learning medium in classrooms, both in principle as well as in recognition of the powerful results achieved by some individual teachers. Yet the use of drama remains rare at best in classrooms and many attempts by teachers remain problematic. My own work with teachers suggests that most teachers have had little exposure to drama as a learning medium and are thus uncertain about how to start, how to structure activities, and so on.

At the heart of the issue, I believe, is the challenge to many teachers implied in improvisational drama of teaching in a different way, a way that *evokes* from children rather than *directs* them, as well as a way that uses new tools of dramatic and theatrical conventions rather than the usual classroom tools for teaching. Such a major shift requires some clear support, I often find, in the form of a protocol, or structure, which provides a larger framework or series of steps within which to work, but which also provides "space" within that framework for improvisation and unplanned possibilities.

The FF technique provides such a protocol that balances structure and openness, starting points and possibilities, directing and evoking, and that can provide teachers with the confidence necessary to begin implementing the approach. Herein lies much of its potential: with this technique, teachers can begin using drama to facilitate student's learning across the curriculum.

Improvisational Drama as a Learning Medium

Improvisational drama has several characteristics which make it an important, and relatively unique, means of learning for pupils in school. The FF technique (described in greater detail elsewhere in this volume) shares in these key characteristics. Hence, its potential value as a learning medium across the curriculum.

Most importantly, improvisational drama, through its use of time and place changes the learner's relationship with what is to be learned, creating a far more personal "here and now" stance toward new information. As the renowned drama educator, Dorothy Heathcote (1983), explains:

> What's possible with drama has to do with the way time is used in drama. Much learning tends to be what I'd call "over there" learning. In other words, when we say, "Let's consider that matter or those people," we are "here" (in time and space) pondering on the matters "over there." But in drama you can't do that, because suddenly you are walking in the time of the event.
>
> For example, let's say we are considering with some children General Wolfe at the siege of Quebec. If we say, "Interesting what Wolfe did at Quebec, wasn't

it?" he remains "over there." Even if we become very involved and intrigued by our study of it, we're still "here" looking "over there."

But in drama the "over there" becomes "here" and the whole world is around me. In this example, it happens to be Wolfe's world at Quebec. Now I'm in a totally different position for joining things together or learning within drama. I can see things only from the point of view of my present responsibility at Quebec. That imminent pressure activates or harnesses my previous knowledge in a totally different way, and very quickly at that. Wolfe is standing there and everyone is saying, "Give us your orders." The historical facts may be vague or even wrong, but the need for Wolfe to suddenly recognize his responsibility can come only through that imminent pressure "here." (p. 695)

Such a basic shift in a learner's relationship with new information is of central importance within a language across the curriculum approach to teaching. Seminal work on children's learning (notably Vygotsky 1962, 1978) as well as numerous studies of classroom instructional practice have revealed a major gap between, on the one hand, the way in which children have shaped their personal experience into knowledge and use it to approach new learning and, on the other hand, how school tends to formulate and shape the public knowledge (in math, science, social studies, and so on) which children come to school to learn. As constructivist learning theory reveals, children can come to understand new information only from the base of what they already know.

This *personal knowledge of children* is largely shaped through a *narrative* structure characterized by *concrete specifics* and laced with *value judgments*.

Public knowledge in school, on the other hand, is usually shaped in an *explanatory, or theoretical*, mode, characterized by *generalities and abstractions* and presented as if it were *neutral*, that is, not in favour of or against anyone.

This gulf between learner experience and school knowledge is strikingly-and humorously-revealed in the following exchange between Caroline and her teacher in a London high school social studies class. Students have been studying the concept of social class and are working on learning material in small groups in the classroom. A confusion arises in Caroline's group and the teacher soon arrives to try to address it.

Caroline: Miss…Miss.

Pupil A: Social classes means upper classes, right?

Observer: Well, all the classes are social classes together.

Pupil A: Oh.

Observer: You know.

Pupil A: And the kind of school we go to?

Observer: Yeh, what kind?

Pupil A: We go to a social class school.

Observer: Well, every . . . what kind, what social class comes to this school?

Caroline: Oh, middle class, um.

Pupil A: Do we . . .?

Caroline: Middle, we are all middle class.

Pupil B: I'm not. I'm poor.

Caroline: You're middle class, you.

Pupil C: We, we're working people.

Caroline: I'm not, I'm not lower class.

Teacher: I'll tell you what, it's a very difficult thing to talk.. . .

Pupil A: We're working class.

Teacher:...about class because you can look at it from two different ways, well, lots of different ways, but two main ways. Firstly, how other people see you.

Caroline: 'Cause there's people worse than us.

Teacher: Yes, it's not a question of better or worse so much. The main thing...

Caroline: I ain't working class.

Teacher: One of the things we talked about, right, when we were looking at social class-you remember this guy I talked about, the registrar general? He has a list of different kinds of jobs that people do and by this list he puts people into different classes. So you have people like professors, the bowler hatters, businessmen, *etc.*, in the class number one, the upper class. In class two you get people like teachers, managers, right, in class two. In class three you get skilled manual workers and then you get unskilled manual workers. Now mainly it's certain kinds of (disruption). That is, he would tend to say that working class people normally have manual skilled jobs, unskilled, semi-skilled jobs, or non-manual jobs, right? But it can be that you have people from the working class that have very, very skilled jobs. Okay, it's a very, very rough, very crude definition.

Caroline: But we're still not working class.

Teacher: And as Caroline says, that a lot of it depends as well on how you see your position in the class system.

Caroline: Maybe you are lower class, I'm not.

Teacher: All right?

Caroline: I'm not.

Teacher: I mean it gets . . .

Caroline: We got a house so we can't be lower class.

Teacher: Well, I haven't, but what does that make me?

Caroline: Peasant. (laughter)

(Searle, 1980)

The long explanation by the teacher in this transcript seems prototypically school-like-abstract, general, categorical, jargon-laden, dry, even numbing, some would claim. Harsh critics would even claim that knowledge-shaped, and "languaged," in this way sucks the life out of life as students know it, rendering their own experience foreign to them. Caroline's grounding in the facts of her own life, such as home ownership, as well as her resistance to what she perceives as the harsh value judgment of being labeled lower class seem to make it almost impossible for her to internalize the way this school knowledge has been shaped. This is not to suggest necessarily that students should not eventually be able to easily handle such school knowledge. However, all too often students have had difficulty bridging the gap between what they know-as well as how they know it-and the new information they are encountering in school, largely because school has, as Barnes (1992) says, expected students "to arrive without having traveled" from where they are starting. Thus, for many students, much of school knowledge has remained at best poorly understood, parroted back from short-term memory, and soon forgotten-- or at worst foreign, confusing, and impenetrable.

Language across the curriculum, briefly, is a pedagogical approach designed to support children in this journey toward internalized learning, toward joining the club of public knowledge in society. It seeks to provide this support by actually directing children back to their personal knowledge as a starting point for new learning and by encouraging their use of "expressive language" (Britton, 1970) as their major means of locomotion for travel. "Expressive language" is the form or style of language closest to what any of us already knows and how we know it. In other words, it is probably the language in which we feel most ourselves. Yet it is also the means by which we can come to understand new concepts, and eventually the public language in which they are formulated. Barnes calls this approach to teaching an *Interpretation* approach (contrasted with school's traditional *Transmission* approach), characterized especially by what he calls "action knowledge" on the part of the student (as opposed to the traditional "boundaried knowledge" of school). Action knowledge, according to Barnes, is created by learners putting school knowledge to applied use in ways that tap into, or activate, students' already existing personal knowledge, thus forging schematic links with the new information of school. When this process works well, students come to internalize school knowledge, but with a strong personal orientation. The following discussion among a small group of fifth graders in social studies seems to be a good example of the creation of *action knowledge* as the students use together what they know to try to come to terms with how the world understands strikes. They have read and discussed a number of newspaper clippings, both news reports as well as opinion pieces, about several current strikes in their city. They have now been asked by their teacher to come up with a definition of a strike, a very school-like concept.

Liz: Sally, what do you think a strike is?

Sally: Okay. A strike is when people . . . okay. A strike is when people are very concerned about . . . something about their jobs . . . Like just say it was like the same with the bus drivers . . . and uh . . . it's a . . . okay, like they want more . . . they want more pay and so they won't go back on work until their . . . until they actually do get higher pay . . . and so um . . . what a strike is is when somebody . . .when people want something changed in their job, they won't work until um . . . until they get what they want.

Liz: You mean like . . . um . . . you . . . you don't think that the work you're doing is getting enough money?

Sally: Right. Yeah. And if you belong to a union . . . like even if you're . . . you feel okay with your job . . . you might have a um . . . most people . . . most jobs do have a union and so they say to go on strike . . . so . . . that's just the facts . . . I think what a strike is.

Luke: You don't have to.

Sally: Yes, if you belong to a union . . . the union says to go on strike . . . the union decides to go on strike . . . because almost if you don't . . . they can take you to court there and they can sue you and everything.

Luke: I'd just quit.

Liz: Okay, mmm . . . Joan, what do you think a strike is?

Joan: Well, I think a strike is when you don't want to do something because somebody says, "Hey, we haven't been getting enough pay . . . getting really . . ." Say somebody in Calgary goes on strike, when they're getting more money . . . and they got their way . . . they . . . they are gonna go cause we're in Alberta and we're gonna go on strike and we're gonna copycat and . . . er . . . say, "Well, we'd be happy to get more money" so they go on strike.

Liz: Joan, you're saying . . . that . . . in Calgary, that one union in Calgary goes on strike . . . and they get . . . you know . . . higher wages and everything . . . then Edmonton's going to copy them, so they can get higher wages?

Joan: No, they're not going to copy them. They're just going to say, "Well, how come they, they're a smaller city, and they're getting more pay and they have less citizens and stuff than us, so why can't we get more pay," so they're gonna go on strike.

Sally: Well, that's not . . . that doesn't concern striking . . . it's just concerned with their jobs . . . like . . . well, you know . . .and there's something they don't like with their job and they want it all fixed up and the people won't fix it up, they'll just go on strike until they do fix it up.

Liz: Okay, um . . . Luke, what do you think a strike is?

Luke: It's when eh . . . when they're asking for more money and . . . complaining 'cause they're not being treated right either . . . I guess that what it is. What do you think?

Liz: If the union decides, "Hey, we're doing all this stuff and they're not paying us, we should get what we deserve" or (yeah) "We work too long" or "We're teachers, we don't . . . we have too many students, you know we can't do that" . . . and so they're just . . .

?: And in support of (unclear)

?: They will teach more students if they get more pay or . . . students.

Sally: Yeah (laughs) . . . $125 dollars a day. Okay, so eh . . .number 2.

(Berry, 1980)

In this example, the children seem to arrive at an accurate and strong understanding of strikes and some of the key issues surrounding them. But note how they "arrived" at that understanding through creating their own concrete narratives in their own expressive language. At one point, the children even tap into the value-laden human issues at work within the framework of strikes, as Luke says he would quit (perhaps as what he sees as unjust power in the hands of a union?) rather than be forced, legally, into what to do. A strike is hardly a neutral notion, no matter how much a school definition may sound that way.

It is noteworthy how "dramatic" is children's natural predisposition to learning, even in discussion, as they create scenarios, or stories, as a major means of making sense of new information. Improvisational drama, although infrequently used in schools, also shares these key characteristics of children's stance toward new information—narration, concreteness, the tension of human issues—and as such is well suited to the needs of students in traveling toward fuller understanding of new ideas. Furthermore, by tapping into what they already know as they engage in dramatic improvisation, children create action knowledge, bringing school ideas to life in an immediate and applied way. Finally, improvisational drama does far more than help children learn the kind of collection of facts, processes, and principles that school usually teaches. It can also expose the issues that lie between people—conflicts, motivations, *etc.*—and can thus help create an "issues-based" approach to curriculum. The following excerpt from a dramatic activity with ten-year-olds on life in a medieval monastery occurred as part of a unit of study in history. It centers on the issue of the monks trying to impose Christianity on the surrounding pagan population. It illustrates well these characteristics of learning through improvisational drama, above all, how "over there" information can become "here and now" understanding.

(Sound of wind and rain sets the scene. The villagers huddle together to discuss their plight.)

Villager 1: There's only one sack-full of corn left, and the crops won't be ready to harvest now until at least a month's time.

Villager 2: Without corn we can't eat bread.

Villager 3: We'll starve.

Villager 1: This corn won't last long—we'll have to do something about it. We must pray to the sun god to give us sun.

Teacher (as villager): But we're not supposed to do that!

Villager 1: Do it in secret then. What have the monks done? *Their* god hasn't done anything—he sent this rain.

Villager 2: Yes—trust in God the monks tell us—but what happens?

Villager 4: Well, I don't know about anybody else but I'm going to pray to the sun god.

The villagers make their way to the mountain to pray to the stone that symbolizes their sun god. During their incantations, the monks arrive and angrily intervene.

Monk 1: Pagans—how dare you pray to that! (*Throwing down altar*)

Villager: We can pray to who we like.

Monk 2: You have sinned! Do you know you are praising a stone? What can a stone do for you?

Crowd: (*muttering*) We've tried praying to your God . . . we can pray to who we like . . . *etc.*

Monk: May God in heaven help them.

Teacher (as villager): Now listen to us . . . our cornfield is ruined. We've come to every service you've asked us to and still our cornfield is wet. That stone is an old stone—a sacred stone—stone older than any man can remember.

Monk: Every stone is old.

Teacher: That stone has stood on this mountainside since men were here.

Monk: I'll tell you what God gives you, you've all been wondering what God does do. That stone can't do what God can . . . he can give you eternal life and make you live again and again.

Teacher: If I can live twice I will worship your God.

(Mallett and Newsome, 1970, pp.54-56)

Granted that, while children's discussion and their improvisational drama share many learning characteristics, a new element is added in improvising, namely the element of "pretend", of taking on the role of another, and especially of giving more "space" to the role of emotions in the human issues which drive any story. Faced with this prospect, many teachers without much experience in drama may worry about inadvertently tapping into painful or difficult emotions on the part of some students, particularly if family dynamics are involved. Clearly, any teacher, whether using drama or not, needs to create an atmosphere of trust and safety in the classroom in order to maximize students' learning. Such an atmosphere is the basis for making effective any kind of interactive learning strategy, from discussion groups to class presentations to dramatic improvising. Beyond this general proviso, dramatic improvising has some "built-in" safety features that ensure a basic level of protection in the classroom.

First, even very young children are quite aware of the difference between fantasy (or "pretend") and reality. Simply observe young children play with dolls or action figures and you will see them move in and out of role easily-and with great awareness. Older learners hardly lose this sense, but rather become even more aware of it. Second, teachers can take steps to create a sense of physical, emotional, and intellectual "distance" from the playing - from constantly indicating to students that what they are doing is fiction or drama and that characters are imaginary, of constantly going in and out of role (and signalling that shift) as developments in the drama warrant, and of developing the ability to step back after the playing to assess and evaluate it in a self-reflective way. All these techniques point continually to the fact that "we are doing drama now".

In short, drama is actually a relatively safe way to deal with human issues, usually much safer than the real-life experiences of children (often just outside classroom doors in school corridors, or playgrounds, or on the way home from school) that are rife with real consequences for them, unlike drama. Dramatic experience can also provide some insight or perspective on human relations as well as some awareness of self that may actually make it possible for children to deal with real-life experiences in a more effective and self-aware fashion. Dorothy Heathcote once offered the opinion that school should be a "safe bower" from which children could explore life. Drama is one means that can make that pedagogical ideal a reality.

From the beginnings of the language across the curriculum movement in the early 70s to the present day, the tradition of drama as a learning medium across the curriculum has continued to develop. It has been spearheaded by the work of several key drama educators -- Dorothy Heathcote (Heathcote & Bolton 1995, Johnson & O''Neill 1984, Wagner 1976) and Gavin Bolton (Bolton 1976, 1984, 1992) in the UK, Cecily O'Neill (O'Neill, 1995, (O'Neill, 1995, O'Neill and Lambert 1984) in the UK and the US, and Norah Morgan and Juliana Saxton (Morgan & Saxton 1987), David Booth (Booth 1994) and Patrick Verriour and Carold Tarlington (Verriour & Tarlington 1991) in Canada. The use of the FF technique for learning across the curriculum contributes another dimension to this tradition of development.

The Fictional Family as a Learning Medium Across the Curriculum

The FF technique reflects many of the characteristics of improvisational drama referred to earlier and can thus be easily adapted as a learning medium across the curriculum, usually through greater predetermination of topic and context than originally conceived for the technique.

General Principles

The original development and use of the FF technique focused a great deal on the character development of individual family members and the interrelationships among those family members. This aspect could be referred to as the dynamics *within* the family unit. Of course, the family created and improvised through this technique also exists in a particular context of time, place, and larger social events-*outside* the family unit. The dynamics within the family can be affected by this context to a greater or lesser extent, depending on the particular characters developed and the conflicts that emerge. However, the particular conflicts and issues that do occur among family members often depend on what individual characters happen to improvise.

In contrast, much use of the FF technique across the curriculum will require greater predetermination by the teacher of several possible aspects of the drama to ensure its "fit" with curricular content. *Within* the family dynamics, a teacher may need to specify the particular issue or conflict to be developed or even at times the identity of family members for the drama. On the other hand, there may be times when the teacher will specify the social context *outside* the family-of time, place, and larger events-as the basis for dramatic tension in the playing.

Furthermore, the use of the FF technique will almost always be a complement to learners encountering curricular information in the classroom in the usual ways-through the reading of texts, by hearing explanations, by watching videos, through engaging in demonstrations, *etc.* However, there is a great deal of flexibility about where the drama might fit in a larger instructional sequence. The FF technique can be a means by which learners activate their relevant personal knowledge *before* encountering school information or a means of applying and internalizing school information by using it in drama *after* having encountered it through reading, listening, or viewing or a mix of both approaches.

Finally, since the FF technique will be one of just several learning means used by teachers around particular curricular content within certain time constraints, teachers will need to pick and choose which of the FF scenes will best apply in their particular situations and not use the entire gamut of FF work willy-nilly or as a matter of course. For example, the activity of Fictional Family Houses may be important for helping students consider the impact of different times and places on the fictional family's living conditions or possibilities. As another example, the activities of the Fictional Family Ten Years Ago or the Fictional Family Ten Years in the Future may well reveal the origins of current issues, the future implications of present-day decisions, or the effects on families of social movements over time. As a final example, Your Fictional Family Character's Dream or Nightmare may be an important activity to supplement learner's explorations of characters in literature or in the creative writing they are producing. Ultimately, a teacher must decide which activities will best suit his or her curricular goals, time constraints, and learners' age and developmental level.

Specific Subject Areas
In light of these general guidelines for adapting the FF technique for classroom learning, let's take a closer look at possible subject-specific

applications of the technique across the curriculum, starting with what might seem to be the more obvious areas.

English Language Arts.

The FF technique adjusts easily to the language arts, the major home of story in the curriculum. Pupils work in a realm of story as they read literature and as they write creatively.

One major way to adapt this technique to language arts is to use it much as originally intended, but then to move on from the characters and families created dramatically and to use them as the basis for fictional writing of various kinds. Inventing dramatically and collaboratively first should provide a strong "running start" of ideas and insights for students' fictional writing, whether poetry, prose, or play writing.

A second application of the technique would be to apply it to already-existing literary characters in a short story, novel, or play (as opposed to creating a fictional family "from scratch"). Such a use of the technique would help students use their imagination to understand much of the implicit aspects of a character's personality, history, and relationships. It would further help them to identify with literary characters, a key quality in becoming a strong literary reader. And it should enable them to delve deeply into the meaning and issues of a story.

Beyond mother tongue development in English, the FF technique would also apply to English as a Second Language education, particularly by providing a broader range of contexts (from informal to formal) and purposes (from informing to persuading to entertaining) for language use than is usually available in the daily life of classrooms.

Moral and Religious Education.

Another obvious area of application of the FF technique is in Moral and Religious Education since tension around moral dilemmas, conflicting values, and so on is often at the heart of drama. The FF technique could be used to explore, not the simplistic role playing of applying a moral code in a "right answer" fashion in a particular situation (i.e., not in a didactic fashion), but rather the true moral, ethical, and value dilemmas that human beings face so often in complex situations. These dilemmas could be faced within a family (e.g., a child torn between conflicting expectations or demands by two parents, or a dilemma raised by one member questioning a family's religious code) or outside the family (*e.g.*, deciding how to act ethically and responsibly in the face of a community issue). The FF technique could also be used comparatively to explore how families from different religious or spiritual backgrounds might approach and respond in the face of the same moral issue.

Social Studies.

Another curriculum area to which the FF technique can be easily adapted is the social studies component of history, geography, economics, civics, *etc*. History is probably the most obvious area in which to apply the technique. It may not lend itself well to exploring the major figures of history, such as kings, generals, or prime ministers, since immediate family relations and dynamics rarely played a part in historical events (although there certainly are exceptions). However, the FF technique could be used to explore the effect of historical events and movements on ordinary families and, thus, the significant meanings of those events on social changes. For example, the Depression caused disruption in the lives of many families-reduced financial circumstances, forced migration, even family break-up, as well as cooperative efforts to help each other. Any of these aspects of that time period could be a crisis-inducing situation for a fictional family of the time. World War II brought about not only the departure of many young men for military service overseas, but also led to greater racial equality and greater employment opportunities for women. Imagine the situation of a fictional family before, during, and after the war. Fictional families of different ethnic and racial origins, as well as different social classes and regions, could expose different perspectives on historical events, as well as the differing effects of those events.

Beyond the area of history, fictional families could face issues of human geography (*e.g.*, choices for making a living based on local natural resources, geography, or population distribution), economics (*e.g.*, the existence of a family farm threatened by the emergence of large agribusiness conglomerates), or civics (*e.g.*, a family involved in a social issue that exposes the need for but also the difficulties of active, democratic citizenship).

In short, social studies is a subject area ripe for exploring social issues and their significance through the specific prism of individual families in various times and places.

Science and Technology.

The FF technique, or any approach to drama in education for that matter, applies not to basic scientific facts and principles *per se*, but rather to the impact of those facts and principles on the daily lives and decisions of individuals, families, and communities. For example, an ecological perspective on science raises issues of how individuals and families in our society contribute to damaging the ecology of the planet (*e.g.*, through the polluting effects of certain lifestyles) or are affected by ecological disturbances or hazards (*e.g.*, individuals who suffer from environmental diseases, farmers threatened by erosion and soil depletion, *etc.*). Technological advances also create issues for individuals and families, from artificial insemination to genetic engineering to the social effects of video games, television, and computers.

Mathematics.

Math may seem like an unlikely area for the use of any drama techniques as ways of learning. However, if we consider the application of math in the social issues that families face and struggle with in daily life, then dramatic possibilities for fictional families begin to open up. For example, a family often faces decisions-and tensions-around living within a certain income and deciding on who gets what, mortgage rates, vacations, debt, *etc.* Family members belonging to a union may face decisions about voting to strike or not on the basis of how far their salary has fallen behind inflation or other sectors of an industry. Citizens may face decisions of how to act in response to government budgetary decisions cutting welfare payments, increasing taxes, or explaining itself with statistics that may distort reality. All these issues involve basic mathematical processes of addition, subtraction, multiplication, and division, but also fractions and percentages, various projections (*e.g.*, how long would it take to pay off this debt if we paid this much per month *versus* that much?), and different ways to represent-and shape-reality through mathematical language, including charts and graphs. Note, however, that these situations also include at their heart human issues involving dilemmas, conflicting values, and resolutions to arrive at-in other words, the essence of drama.

An Interdisciplinary or Issues-based Curriculum.

This subject-by-subject review of the possible applications of the FF technique in various areas of the curriculum reveals not only the single-subject uses of the technique, but also suggests an interdisciplinary, or issues-based, approach to the curriculum. If we place the dynamic and conflicts of fictional family members within a deliberate social context of time, place, and larger forces, we see that the issue at the centre of the drama often includes a mix of subject areas. For example, the situation of a fictional family facing a threat to the financial viability of a family farm in a certain area because of changes in the physical environment and/or because of the emergence of large, agribusiness competition, includes content from science (ecological concerns of soil erosion, climate change, *etc.*) and technology (large-scale farming techniques), from mathematics (efforts to survive financially in the face of debt, mortgage payments, income, *etc.*), from social studies (government decisions that might favour big business over family enterprises, the role of citizens in shaping and responding to those decisions, *etc.*), and possibly even historical background to a situation and how it has changed over time or could change in the future. Even related literature, such as Jane Smiley's *A Thousand Acres*, could enrich the exploration of an issue like this, as well as help students gain insight to a novel like that.

An additional note about the language arts in particular: While certain subject areas may or may not be present in a particular drama, the language arts will always be present since students will be at least talking in role. A great deal of the dramatic activity will be oral, but there can be many possibilities for reading and writing in role (what Myra Barrs, 1987, calls "drama on paper"). Learners in role can read documents from another time, such as newspapers, or current resources like government pamphlets or company reports. On the other hand, learners may write in role, as they compose letters to distant family members (*e.g.*, to a son who has gone off to war) or to newspaper op-ed pages or to elected officials about social issues. Even media, such as film, video, or television could be viewed in role when appropriate. In this way, all the language arts-listening, speaking, reading, writing, and viewing-can be used and developed in drama in all subject areas in a truly across-the-curriculum fashion.

Multi-cultural Education

Certain key guiding principles for education cut across all subject areas and would ideally pervade all aspects of classroom life. One such key principle is multi-cultural education, defined as an approach to education that strives for equity and social justice in relation to all differences in power linked with social groupings, such as gender, race, class, ability, religion, sexual preference, and so on. This educational approach strives first for a greater awareness of these issues of power between groups and their pervasive presence in relationships among people. This pedagogy will then often use this new awareness as a springboard for taking action toward social justice, or equity, in some particular realm, such as gender or race, *etc.*

These issues of social discrimination can be dealt with in two ways in the school. The first is to embed the pedagogy in a subject area itself so that the teaching exposes these issues. For example, a history class might look deliberately at the situation, the response by, and the effect on various social groups (*e.g.*, the poor, women, blacks, *etc.*) of a particular event (*e.g.,* the Depression or World War II). Or an English course could use literature to explore male-female relations in various times and places, including here and now. The second approach is to directly address the actual issues that affect the social health of students in a classroom, a school, or a neighbourhood, such as racism or sexism. In short, this approach to education acknowledges that all knowledge and interaction is essentially social in nature and, thus, is always gendered, raced, classed, and so on and tries to work within that awareness. Once again, the FF technique lends itself well to exploring these issues of discrimination either within a curriculum area or directly as it affects a group of learners.

Looking Ahead

I have explored the potential and promise of improvisational drama for learning in school, in particular the FF technique. While the technique shares much of the potential for learning that all drama does, it also holds much promise since it is based on perhaps the most basic aspect of our experience, namely family life. As such, it can provide the kind of dramatic situations that teachers as well as students should be able to relate to easily. Finally, the kinds of meaning and significance found in a fictional family context should help make the all-too-foreign information encountered by learners in school much closer to what and how they already know. In short, it should help students feel "at home" with school learning and, thus, to learn well.

References

Barnes, Douglas. *From Communication to Curriculum* (2nd editions). Portsmouth, NH: Boynton/Cook, Heinemann, 1992.

Barrs, Myra. Voice and Role in Reading and Writing. *Language Arts*, 64, 2: 207-218, 1987.

Berry, Kathleen The Oral Language and Learning of Grade 5 Students. Unpublished Master's thesis, University of Alberta, 1982.

Bolton, Gavin. Toward a Theory of Drama in Education. London: Longman, 1979.

_____. New Perspectives on Classroom Drama. London: Simon & Shuster, 1992.

Booth, David. Story Drama. Markham. ON. Pembroke Publishers, 1994.

Britton, James. *Language and Learning*. Harmondsworth, Mdsx: Penguin, 1970.

Heathcote, Dorothy. Learning, Knowing, and Languaging in Drama: An Interview with Dorothy Heathcote. *Language Arts*, 60, 6, 695-701, 1983.

Johnson, Liz, and O'Neill, Cecily (Eds.). Dorothy Heathcote: Collected Writings on Education and Drama. London: Hutchison, 1984.

Mallett, Margaret, and Newsome, Bernard. *Talking, Writing, and Learning 8-13*. London: Evans/Methuen Educational, 1970.

Morgan, Norah, and Saxton, Juliana. Teaching Drama. London: Hutchison, 1987.

O'Neill, Cecily. *Process Drama*. Portsmouth, NH: Heinemann, 1995.

O'Neill, Cecily, and Lambert, Alan. *Drama Structures*. London: Hutchison, 1984.

Searle, Dennis. *The Language of Adolescents In and Out of School*. Unpublished doctoral dissertation, University of London, 1981.

Muriel Gold, C.M., Ph.D.

Verriour, Patrick, and Tarlington, Carol. *Role Drama.* Markham, ON: Pembroke Publishers, 1991

Vygotsky, Lev. *Language and Thought.* Cambridge, MA: MIT Press, 1962

_____. *Mind in Society.* Cambridge, MA: Harvard University Press, 1978.

Wagner, Betty Jane. *Dorothy Heathcote: Drama as a Learning Medium.* Washington, DC. National Education Association, 1976.

Chapter Three:

Writing across the Curriculum through Drama

Judy Kalman

> Our knowledge of the world is inextricably bound up with the way we *feel* about the world, about people and things and events and ourselves. Our ways of feeling, taken overall, show a persistent patterning which constitutes our value system. It is our values that make us the sort of people we are, and it is on the basis of shared values that we establish our most intimate network of relationships with other people. To define learning as *coming to know* something about the world that we did not know before, while denying the term to *change in the way we evaluate some experience* is to make a false disjunction.
>
> (Barnes, Britton, Torbe, 105-6)

My parents were born teachers, and my first "college" was our dining-room table. My parents were also models of "lifelong learners"; that was their philosophy. They lived it in their own lives and led their children, my brother and myself, along the same exciting path.

At five years old, I was a teacher, modelling my classroom on my parents' dining-room. I taught my dolls in a basement classroom, putting them in a circle so that they could help each other as well as "discuss" with me. I rewarded their contributions, both right and wrong, with an "Isn't that interesting!" This was my expectation of school, although I couldn't articulate it at the time.

Reality was somewhat less kind. Stultifying, deadening, disempowering, boring. The kind of experience that made me want to stay in bed with the sheet over my head. I was in the advanced class, gifted *before* the term was defined and accepted in popular parlance. But to the teachers in my school, gifted meant docile memorization (without necessarily understanding the concept), regurgitation of information, good grades, and respect (for them, not for us) Play an off-note in the orchestra, and bear the brunt of excruciating notice and sharp comment; never mind that you had always wanted to play an instrument and felt like Yitzhak Perlman. And how long could your secret dream survive the scathing tongue of the music teacher? Miss the basket too many times, or hit the net with the volleyball once too often, and you never received any support from your classmates or your gym teacher in your quest to be physically active and healthy. Write a composition as a poem and have the wrath of the teacher descend upon you like the thunderbolt of an angry Zeus. You weren't original or questing; you were a smart aleck. You thought you were Tennyson, but you were only a student who needed taking down a peg or two. Questioning, critiquing (in the true sense of the word), understanding, critical thinking--these made you a troublemaker. I tuned out, my grades sank lower each year, and by the time I graduated in the eleventh grade, I felt I was *not* intelligent. I failed geometry, and just passed algebra and chemistry.

What did I learn? I learned that I was wrong most of the time, and that I couldn't learn. My self-esteem was hitched to memorizing Alfred

Noyes' *The Highwayman*, and the only line that I remembered was "Tlot, tlot". I had a reputation for "conceit" with two of my teachers because I asked why I couldn't write/solve problems this way rather than that. I could feel, as the years passed by, my anxiety level increasing, day by day, test by test, class by class, and I learned to drink coffee and to smoke cigarettes as a way to ward off the demons of academe. I loved the give and take of discussions at my family dinner table and I eagerly participated on the battleground, but the feeling that pervaded the bulk of my life, as school pervaded the bulk of my life, of not being appreciated, of being misunderstood, of being the catnip of the class with various cats ready to pounce on me at a moment's notice, stifled all the creativity, excitement, sharing, experimenting that was in me. Learning was for conversation at home; school was a test of my survival skills, and I came oh so close to dying in the wilderness.

My experience as a student often reappears in my conversations with students, and has left me with an awareness of what encourages students and what disempowers them. I see nervous students in the first days of a composition or literature class. They feel they can't write, and they don't want to be there. What if they embarrass themselves in front of the class and the teacher "shoots them down" or worse, their classmates laugh? They don't want to hand in work; they can't create and they are not creative. To leave students feeling this way throughout the semester is a recipe for defeat for a significant number of students.

The Fictional Family

I am constantly searching for new ways to make writing exciting for my students and to bridge the gap between writing and knowledge in other areas. And I have discovered that ideas appear in the most unlikely places. That is why I was not overly surprised to learn about one of the techniques that I have come to use the most in a small article on a back page of a community newspaper.

It was the words "fictional family" which drew my attention: "fictional" because fiction is part of what I teach, and "family" because that is, in part, my classroom philosophy. As I read about Muriel Gold's method of creating a family construct within the university drama class, I began to spin exciting scenarios of how I could use this method to teach rhetorical modes to my students, how it would lend itself to descriptive, narrative, and even persuasive writing, and how students could stretch their abilities within the security of a self-created, nurturing environment. This small newspaper article was an invitation to begin one of the most exciting experiences of my teaching career; in a few paragraphs, here was the suggestion of a method that would address all my teaching goals: effective writing instruction; confidence-building; and writing across the curriculum. Looking at the technique from a purely pedagogic viewpoint, I had no idea what excitement FF would engender in students from all disciplines, from fine arts to business, an excitement which it has been and is a satisfaction to encounter. What I did know was that I wanted to bridge the gap between my students' lives and learning, between the skills they thought they had and the skills I knew that they could develop:

> All human beings experience life on the basis of their own cultural values and assumptions, most of which are outside their awareness. Unless confronted by others whose values differ from our own, we inevitably see the world through our own 'cultural filters', often persisting in established views despite clear information to the contrary. Ethnicity is deeply tied to the family through which it is transmitted.
>
> (Monica McGoldrick,
> quoted in Gold,
> *English Quarterly*, 29)

Students come to schools and universities with a self-knowledge based on who they are and from where they come. Are they willing and able to break down the barriers to new ways of seeing? Are they able, in dialogue with others, to work through strongly held beliefs gained in their environments, a world-view which means "safety", to accept the very different ideas of others? Do they even realize that they have a set of assumptions and values through which they analyze life? The comparison of ideas/responses is a crucial step in learning. Comparing one's ideas, values, and world view with others is the only way of measuring one's growth, and indeed stimulates that growth, and validates the direction in which one is moving.

In the Contemporary Jewish Literature Classroom:

In my Survey of Contemporary Jewish Literature course, given to students at the college level, most of those who are in the class are not Jewish. They have no idea that there *is* Jewish writing, except as it pertains to the Holocaust: Anne Frank and Elie Wiesel, or the conflict in the Middle East about which they read in the newspapers. They have little knowledge of the culture and the religion, and while they feel it is strangely exotic, they are also worried about their ability to grasp the meaning of readings so alien to their experience. In the course, these students are exposed to short stories, novels and poems written by Jewish writers on Jewish themes. They use the FF to help them make meaning out of their readings, to build bridges between the Jewish experience and their own.

After reading several pieces of short fiction and two novels, the students create any family they want, with the one guideline that the family must mirror at least one of the themes in the course. Many students choose the theme of immigration, one that resonates in their own lives and those of their families.

Muriel Gold, C.M., Ph.D.

Selected Fictional Family Themes

Immigration

The Kristovs are a family who have immigrated to Canada from Russia. They are Catholic, and the children are cared for by their father, as their mother has died. In this family, the themes of loss and the difficulty of assimilation loom large. Six year old Olga (Diana) writes:

> Mama was very pretty but she's sleeping with the angels now and Papa says that they are taking very good care of her. I look just like Mama, Papa told me so. I have her curls and her green eyes. I also laugh like her and that makes me happy because I have never met her. The angels took her right after I came out of her belly

Every Sunday, Papa puts my coat on and takes my hand and we walk to church together. Papa lifts me while I light a candle and pray to baby Jesus to take care of my mama. Sometimes Papa cries but not too much, because he wants to be big and strong. I hold his hand and tell him that Mama told me to tell him that she likes where she is and she has lots of friends to play with. He smiles when I tell him that and that makes me very happy.

Papa and I walk to church together

In this essay, the wistfulness and longing of a child who has lost her mother as well as the pain of a father widowed in a land far from his own is apparent, as is the dependence that these family members have on each other.

Another view of this family is portrayed in the letter that Olga's eldest sister, Helena (Elise), twenty-seven and the "mother" figure, gives to Sophia, seventeen. Sophia has a boyfriend, Bruce Lee, who is approximately her age and not part of her culture or her religion:

> Since you confronted Papa about your relationship
> with Bruce, nothing has been the same in our family.

Everyone is trying to avoid each other; Papa is so tense that he bursts out in anger at anything. It is true that things have changed, and that we are not in Russia anymore. While you now have the right to go out with whomever you like, with your new privileges come new responsibilities and challenges. We still carry the memory of our former home. When you move to a new country, your past isn't wiped clean.

From my observations, Bruce is very kind and honest. I am in agreement that it is unfair to dismiss someone because of his skin colour or his origins. How fortunate we are that our host country didn't refuse us for the same reason!

Nevertheless, I understand Papa's desire to perpetuate our Russian traditions. The cultural heritage of your children should not be neglected when you consider the possibility of having a foreigner as a husband. Will your children speak Russian with a foreign father?

In this piece, Elise deals with one of the thorniest dilemmas of an immigrant: how to keep one's culture and adapt to the culture of his/her new home. All the responsibility of being a "mother", the anguish of being caught between the father and the sister she loves, and the desire that both father and sister be content comes out in this essay.

Holocaust

Fictional family is particularly useful in helping students take up exceptionally difficult themes in literature. While I feel that simulating Holocaust families is neither useful nor valid and I don't encourage it, one group of students was deeply moved by the plight of victims of the Holocaust This group envisaged what would happen to a German family who refused to take part in or to be bystanders to the Nazi persecution of Jews in Germany. The Bicancomers have immigrated to Canada both to save daughter Heidi's fiancee who is Jewish, and to avoid being coerced by the Nazis; the parents are professionals, and Heidi, the older daughter, is preparing to marry. Marta (Falon), a self-professed 15-year-old tomboy, "and a spoiled one", describes her displacement:

> I am German and a Bicancomer, a well-known name in Germany. It is true that our family is a very big one and well-known, but the reason for which they now know us is different. We are considered traitors, simply because we are against their horrendous intentions. It is sad. I love my Germany and in my mind, it is impossible to understand how my people could have such cruel intentions against other races.
>
> I now find myself lost, somehow empty, as if I have lost my identity. "I am Marta Bicancomer"; it doesn't raise that brow anymore, as when people would say, "Oh! Ms. Bicancomer" My family name is part of an identity, but now it doesn't seem like it means much.
>
> I, who have been interested in learning so much about other cultures, am not so thrilled anymore. I asked to learn about them; I never asked to *be* them. My Germany, oh, how much I miss it! "I am Marta Bicancomer", whatever that might mean to you.

The ease with which students, reading stories of the atrocities of the Holocaust, say that *they* would not collaborate with the Nazis, and *they* would prevail, is dispelled in this FF, as they come to realize what the cost of prevailing has been. The loss of identity of the Jewish victims resonates in the minds this family, as they realize just what their country has done and how much the victims have suffered.

Improvisation and Interview Exercises

Along with their FF essays, the students have an improvisation exercise, in which they envision a family meal in their new country. All the stresses and strains come out in these two minutes "onstage", as the families grapple with unfamiliar food, unfamiliar occasions, relationships strained to the breaking point, and outsiders introduced into the fabric of the family.

The FF assignment is joined to the interview assignment, in which students must find and interview a person who has immigrated to Canada. The student then links the experience of the interviewee to the fiction that they have been reading in class, and situates the Jewish experience within the other experiences which they have created and discovered.

This leads to a much fuller integration of the course material with the students' own lives. In their final papers, which plot the students' intellectual journey through the course, they comment on the depth of understanding and attachment they have built between themselves and the literature they have studied. Students feel that they have learned the material in a way that will remain with them, that this is not a course they will walk away from and forget, once the beach beckons.

The Fictional Family and Rhetorical Modes

Steven McCarty is forty years old. He is the butler to a wealthy family in Brazil. Who is he really? He describes himself in his descriptive essay in terms of the food he makes for each member of the family, every one of whom has problems which are reflected in his or her food preferences.

Robby Mail is twenty-six, an artist and the sole support of his family since the death of their parents in a plane crash four years previously. Those he takes care of include his seventeen-year old sister Edith and his young brother Bobby. The problem is "how" Robby supports them all; he is a male stripper. This is particularly problematic because Edith is consumed by religion and Bobby is only ten and sees Robby as a role model.

These two characters were developed by students in a six-week university composition course which teaches rhetorical modes. Students' concerns related to the covering of course material are particularly evident in vastly concentrated courses. Particularly because the course is so compact, students have some valid questions and concerns about the use of this construct in class time which are addressed during the first class and in the ensuing weeks. Of most concern to them are the following:

Am I learning everything I should in the course if so much of the time is consumed by FF?
Does FF have a academic rationale in terms of the course material?
What happens if I don't get along with the people in my fictional family?
I am not a creative person, and am afraid I will not succeed in this part of the course.
Of what use is the FF in my training toward a specific career? and finally,
What will happen if I find the fictional family to have an unbearable resonance with my personal life?

It has been my experience that, after a thorough discussion of the material to be covered and the ways in which the FF helps us to cover it, the students are reassured that they will be learning all they should. As an added assurance, I tell them that the marks of students in my class are equal to or slightly higher than those of students in other sections. They are also assured that accommodation will be made in the event that they do not interact well with their fictional family. Visiting another family for an extended period is one option, and several of the in-class activities facilitate inter-family contact, as, for example, the party scene wherein all the families meet each other at an informal get-together. Moreover, (although I have not yet had this situation in any class), if a student were to have great difficulty with a portion of the FF activities, s/he would be exempted from that part.

The value of the FF, particularly in the shortened summer semester, is that it creates a community in which the student is welcome, an experience which a marginalized student may not have had before. It creates an atmosphere in which the student is free to experiment un-self-consciously in a variety of modes and to learn to work with others, trust others, cooperate with others, and resolve conflicts with others. What better place to accomplish this than in a fictional family?

The "How" of the Fictional Family in the Composition Class

The university-level composition course that I teach is an essay writing course. Its curriculum is aimed at teaching students the rhetorical modes and devices that they will use in essay and report writing both at school and beyond. FF assignments in this course are designed to give students experience in the required modes of writing: description, narration, exposition, and persuasion/argumentation. The assignments are also divided into formal and informal exercises. Three of the five required formal essays are written about the fictional family; students are asked to describe their fictional characters, write a story about an important event in the life of their characters, and to write an essay based on a conflict in their fictional families.

As well, students keep *journals* in which at least half the writing has to do with considering various aspects of their characters, enunciating their beliefs and values, and experimenting with various modes of writing, to fit the various moods of their characters. They propel themselves backward and forward in their characters' lives: My name is _____. I am (10, 45, 80) years old. This particular journal entry takes the students out of the "now" and requires them both to project themselves into the future and to analyze the past of their characters.

Moreover, they look at their actual families, writing on such topics as: What is a family? A mother/father? A grandmother/grandfather? and writing about the most interesting thing about their own families. The movement back and forth, between self and character, gives the students a kaleidoscope of perspectives on family relationships and all that they involve. The result is that often students gain not only an understanding of the principles of writing, but also of the real feelings and dilemmas/ joys/sorrows of people in other stages of life.

The final component of FF in the classroom is the creation of family scenes in class. These dramatic representations encompass a variety of situations and emotions, and involve everyday speech and life experience. The families enact a special occasion in their lives; they reveal a secret; and they have a party with other fictional families. Even those students who are self-conscious become involved in the holiday traditions sabotaged by the "rebellious son" or the revelation that Grandma has had a million dollars hidden away for the last ten years. These interactive opportunities are followed by a period of writing ("ink-shedding") which helps the students sort out what the experience has meant to him/her and how it fits in with his/her conception of his/her character. In this way, the link between spoken language, used outside of the school environment, and the writing done for the course is established.

The Descriptive Essay

Students often think that description is the "easiest" form of writing. Who can't describe something? You look at it, and you write what it looks like, or smells like or sounds like. And yet, finding the organizing principles of a descriptive essay can be difficult.

In the classroom, the students discuss how they will describe their characters. Will they focus on looks? Personality? Character? How will they "make their character jump from the page"? How will they ensure unity and coherence and yet grab the reader's attention and keep it.

Having an actual character to work on, one which is intimately known to the writer, helps invest this piece with meaning.

> I am Maria-Juanita Rodriguez, thirty years old (but I'll deny it if you ask), and beautician extraordinaire. I have the most incredible hair on our block: long; shiny; black; down to my waist. My bod is pretty hot too, if you ask me. So why can't I find a man? No, that's not true. Finding a guy is not the problem; it's finding the *right* one that is.
>
> There's Ricardo, who's been following me since tenth grade. There's also John, the guy whose wife comes to my shop to get her lip waxed; he's kinda cute and I think he does something on Wall Street. It's too bad he's married, but that never seems to matter! Hmmm…Don the musician, Marco the cabbie-I couldn't go for him, he'd probably get shot. Maybe someday I'll have a rich, handsome hunk for a husband and two kids; that's what I want.

Here the writer artfully interweaves physical and emotional characteristics in a complex way. The reader can see the character's lush appearance and feel the desperation for "Barbie's" dream under the surface. The colloquial language adds to our vision of Maria; she sounds just as she is.

The Narrative Essay

In many cultures, the narrative teaches society much of what it needs to know. We are surrounded by narrative: the Bible, the soap operas, commercials. In any college corridor, student conversation is narrative. And yet, in the classroom, narrative is often not rated as a teaching tool: "Ms. Jones is a great teacher, but I think that she should forget about the stories and get on with the material we need to know." Students in my classroom are encouraged to explore what narrative can teach. What is the value of the story? How can a narrative describe a life lesson?

Maria Juanita Rodriguez and her men

As with descriptive writing, so narrative writing seems deceptively easy to produce. In the class, we look at which details to include and which to omit. We discuss pace, where to place the conflict and the climax. How long the end of the story should be. We come to the conclusion that there is a reason that the end of the Cinderella story is "And they lived happily ever after." Does anyone really want to read "And Cinderella and the prince went on a honeymoon to Hawaii where they stayed at the Hilton; After their return home, they had a son, and then a daughter and another son in quick succession; Cinderella had a terrible time finding household help while she was bringing up her children and the prince was not a comfort...?" A group of students write of a family who emigrate to Canada from Ireland; they have chosen to write the narrative as a letter to family back home:

> Dear Auntie Colleen and Uncle James,
> We were all up before dawn the day we planned to leave. I could see through the window that there were no lights shining from within the other homes in the glen. Huddled around the hearth, we were all lost in our own thoughts. It was with mixed feeling that we were leaving. Sadness over leaving the only home we'd ever known, excitement because of the new land we were going to and fear of the unknown.

With this introduction, the writers draw the reader into the preparations for this momentous journey:

> So many plans were discussed, it was enough to make a head ache at the thought of it, through the leave-taking and the harrowing journey to the arrival on a strange shore and all the insecurities attendant on a new life in a new place:
> You're all too smart for me to hand you a lot of blarney, so I won't even try. Life here is not easy. We're lucky. We have work, we have our health and we have each other. Most of all, we have a powerful faith in the

Almighty, which I feel sure will help us through these troubled times. Every Sunday, I make sure we all go to church. Father John has been a big help to us. Britt is his family name. His family is from County Cork. He is a fine priest and a credit to his race.

You all had so many dreams for us and we're working hard to make them come true. The pride and stubbornness we've inherited will serve us well in doing just that…that and a parcel of common sense. It is our hope that before too long we'll be standing at the dock to greet whoever is coming over next. Until then may God bless you and keep you while we hold memories of you close to our hearts. Love always.

In the end of this narrative is all the hardship and loneliness that this family feels in a world so far from the familiar, and all the pride of success in making their way. The tone leaves the reader with conflicting feelings, just as the narrators express conflicting feelings…fear, endurance, hard-won success, and longing all inform this story, and draw us in through our own battles through frightening and lonely experiences.

The Essay of Argument

Students write to a fictional family member with whom they *share a conflict,* that is, both characters view an issue in a substantially different light. The characters might share a conflict over parenting, money, or household responsibilities; the areas for conflict are many. Perhaps the person whom the writer addresses does not recognize the disunity as yet but if lack of agreement is inherent in the issue, there is a shared conflict. Incorporated in this piece of writing is the recipient's point of view and the writer's appreciation and understanding of the recipient's point of view. The body of the essay is controlled by the writer's purpose. Is s/he writing to set forth her/his own position? To have the recipient take the writer's position into consideration? To convince the recipient of the correctness of the writer's position? The purpose is relevant to the essay. And finally, is there a particular solution to the conflict that the writer envisions? Does s/he insist that there be movement of some kind? This exercise takes the student out of his/her point of view and into the thoughts and actions of another person or situation, a valuable exercise in critical thinking.

One of the most difficult endeavours is to argue our point persuasively. In the class, we discuss what types of arguments sway opponents. How do we argue against an entrenched position? What kinds of words do we use?

What is the effect of an *ad hominem* argument (name-calling)? Does it make a difference in what order we place our points? Students begin to discover that holding onto an entrenched position may not be the most successful way to convince someone with an opposing view. They begin to see that "tone" is vital to persuasion. And this leads us to a discussion of the ways that writing mirrors the feelings of the writer and appeals to the feelings of the reader.

In the following excerpt from an essay, a son writes to his father of the conflict that has occurred due to the father's remarriage. He articulates his understanding of the difficulties his father has experienced in bringing up a son as a widowed parent. He articulates his feelings, living in his father's new family, and ends by reaching out to his father to end the estrangement that exists:

> You often commented that while death is inevitable, and often predictable, the sorrow which accompanies such loss never brings advanced warning. I guess you had a feeling that death has a way of changing people and their relationships. Come to think of it, so did I, except I believed that tragedy brings people closer together. I know that you were unprepared to all of a sudden become a single father when Mother passed away. I also understand how difficult it must have been for you to lose your loving

wife. I remember how proud you were of your family. You spoke passionately about wanting another child or two, and buying that split-level cottage which mother liked so much. You had dreams which appeared well on their way to becoming reality, until she died.

...I guess you probably felt that Mother would have wanted you to remarry. Perhaps you thought that I needed a mother-figure to help me overcome my grief. Or maybe your dream of a larger family became an obsession. Whatever the reason, what you didn't count on was that your only son was lost the day your new wife was found.

...We shouldn't pretend that we are comfortable with the tension which exists between us. It appears that all we share now are cold stares and angry words. There are times, I must admit, when I get an aching feeling to talk to you like we used to. Sometimes I childishly rehearse my thoughts, then I catch your eye and quickly look away. Anger provides me with the courage to face you; however, sadness makes me more vulnerable. I don't want to hear your razor-sharp replies anymore. And I am tired of feeling like an unwanted link to a time that you would rather not recall.

...I haven't given up on us yet, but faith alone will not do. This is my way of reaching out to you, as I feel we need each other. And while time has brought us slightly closer together, I realize that time can only do so much.

Here is a carefully crafted argumentative essay, complete with major issue, opponent's point of view and the writer's analysis. Fictional Family conflict is the vehicle by which this student is able to analyze a problem and work it through to a logical conclusion in a persuasive way.

Students, at the end of the semester, are asked to evaluate the FF experience in a written entry in their journals. One student in particular articulated the gamut of learning experiences that students undergo using FF in the composition class. Markos writes:

> My experience with the fictional family has helped me rediscover a creativity I thought I had lost. When I first began the fictional family, I found it difficult to come up with scenarios or any kind of feel for what my character would be like. So I took the easy way out and made him a ridiculous freak. By doing that I thought that it would be obvious what I had to do; he would have to be depressed about his physical appearance and that is what I would do.
>
> I soon realized that it would be more complicated than that. I had to combine his personality with those of the group, especially for the first essay. This became a real problem in the beginning because I don't think anybody had a real feel for their characters. I tried as best I could to gain an understanding of what the others wanted from my character and for what they were going to do with theirs.
>
> The fictional family definitely taught me to listen, as I had to understand quite intimately what the other wanted in a very short amount of time. Then I had to integrate my character with the others, and this was definitely a challenge. But it was nothing compared with having to get a feel for my character, I mean to really establish how he would feel and then to reflect that in the style of writing, as the writing was all in the first person.

Once I had done the first essay, however, I had clearly defined the character in my mind. I was then able to play on his weakness and strength and began to feel the kinds of things he would say. I think the most important thing was to understand that he was my character and so it was up to me to make him whatever I wanted him to be.

Another great thing about that was that it gave me a lot of freedom, which is not something one usually gets in school, to do whatever I wanted with a project....I got to explore some emotion which really should be done, more especially if I am supposed to be studying psychology, which is all about the way people feel. If I did this more often, I would probably make a better psychologist in the future.

...Fictional family allowed me to do some group work in a creative capacity, something we do not get many opportunities to do in a university environment.

In my composition course as well as in my Contemporary Jewish Fiction course, the FF's importance as a learning technique lies in the fact that it "helps students learn language, learn through language, and learn about language" and lends itself to Britton's three categories of writing: transactional, expressive, and poetic. It has little to do with "rote learning" but has much to contribute to "genuine learning", a distinction recognized by Britton in *Language and Learning Across the Curriculum* (221). This leads me full circle from my position as a disenchanted student to my position as excited and eager teacher. The words once booming through a high school classroom: "Judy will never amount to anything", now only occur in the setting of a fictional character in a FF, in an exercise that facilitates learning of rhetoric, fictional modes, and learning across the curriculum.

While a careful analysis of the pedagogic value and effects of the FF in the classroom is both necessary and rewarding, I will leave the last word for my students, who are, after all, both the recipients and benefactors in the classroom:

> "The fictional families gave the students an opportunity to become friends with different people in the class, people who you would normally not have a chance to meet. The exercise was different and it allowed us to be different. New and creative teaching methods are what are needed in our school system. Bravo."

> "The use of fictional families in this course is very beneficial. Within the first couple of classes, it gets students talking and makes them comfortable with others. For this reason alone, the fictional family is very important and helpful. In a composition course of this type-where class participation is imperative to learning the techniques, it doesn't work if everyone is afraid to speak up and voice his or her opinions and ideas."

> "Another reason why the fictional family helps in composition is that it gets students to see past "writing for a grade" and to write for a reason, depending on the assigned topic. It also helps to write in another character, to see another's point of view and to keep from straying away from the topic."

> "This project also gave students the ability to use their imaginations in order to write creatively. Activities which each fictional family engaged in can be experienced not only by university students but by students of any level of education. Therefore, I give the fictional family project two thumbs up!"

"The fictional family gives you the opportunity to think about your family values, your beliefs, and your attitudes toward different people and different situations. I have learned that I am very open-minded in terms of what constitutes a family. Also I am not afraid to express my true feelings about certain issues with people I do not know very well. If no one volunteers to take on the leadership position in the group, I will do so myself. I never thought I had any leadership qualities."

"The fictional family was a most useful creative exercise...removed barriers, and presented endless possibilities for my writing. This does not suggest that my time in the fictional family was all fun and games, as a very distinct aspect of my personality was included in my very strange fictional family member. The concept of the fictional family allowed me the safety to explore situations and take chances with relatively little risk. After all, it wasn't me or my opinions, it was my character's strange personality. The fictional family allowed me to explore interests that I never knew I had, and gave me insight into how I would deal with situations of tremendous stress."

References

Barnes, Douglas, James Britton, Mike Torbe. *Language, the Learner and the School.* Portsmouth, N.H.: Boynton/Cook, 1990.

Barr, Mary and Mary K. Healy. "Language Across the Curriculum." *Handbook of Research on Teaching the English Language Arts.* Ed. James Flood et al. London: Macmillan, 1991.

Gold, Muriel. "The Fictional Family: A Perspective of Many Cultures'. *English Quarterly* 25.2 (Spring, 1993): 26-28.

Chapter Four:

Drama and Creative Writing: Poetry, Playwriting, and Journals

Muriel Gold

A special interest of mine is the use of drama to stimulate creative writing. A number of sessions, therefore, are devoted to providing students with the appropriate stimuli-sensory experiences, character movement,-to provoke imaginative writing. These original texts subsequently become vehicles for the production of students' individual, personal theatre creations. The performance pieces can be acted as monologue, dialogue or in a group.

Blind/Trust Exercise

For example, I will initiate a blind/trust exercise in which students are divided into pairs. One wears a blindfold, the other acts as guide. There are three stages. In the first stage, the guide holds the arm of the "blind" student. During the second stage, the guide stays beside the blind person, vocally alerting h/er about obstacles, but does not hold h/er. During the third stage the guide is further away in the room but they agree in advance on a sound signal which the guide will use if the blind person is in danger. Then they reverse roles so that each student has had an opportunity to experience both being blind and being a guide (Way, 1967).

I will then follow it with a creative imagining exercise in which students are asked to lie down and close their eyes. First, they are led through breathing and relaxation exercises; second, they are asked to recall in every detail what it was like being blind, and also what it was like being guide to the blind person. Third, they are asked to sit up and write a few poetic sentences describing the experience, beginning with "My name is _____. I am blind."

Seated on the floor in a circle, students in turn read their 'poems' to the group. They are then asked to integrate their writing with another student's which may (or may not) contain some element similar to theirs. Out of this combination, the two students create a performance piece. They may add costume pieces, props, music and/or dance, if they wish. The results are often incredibly imaginative, innovative, amusing and moving.

Childhood Memory Exercise

Similar stimuli are initiated for other topics. A second example grows out of what I call Childhood Memories which begins with the students closing their eyes and imagining that they are candles on a giant birthday cake. I ask them to form an image of the cake, of its ingredients, icing, color, taste and smell.

'When you feel a gentle tap on your head, your wick is being lit, and you begin to melt slowly until you become a blob on the cake and you fall over.'

(Objectives: to develop concentration, physical control and sense memory techniques)

While they are lying on the floor, I ask them to recall the birthday parties they have experienced in the various stages of their lives-to recall where they took place, who was there, what they wore, what others wore, what the decor was like, and the sounds, colors, textures, tastes and smells of each environment. I ask them to see these parties as though they had been filmed and they were watching a film of the parties they had attended. Then I ask them to form an image of themselves as a six-year-old child at a birthday party.

'Decide who you are, where you are, who else is there, what you are wearing, when it is taking place, the time of day, of year, what the decor is like, and what you want. Imagine the tastes, smells, colors, textures, sounds of the environment. At the sound of the tambour, rise - you are a six-year-old child at a birthday party.'

(Objectives: To help students prepare for their roles through their own sense memory, their own emotions, their own particular life experiences.)

While the students are moving about the space, they are being prompted to determine who they are, where they are coming from, and why, what they want, where they are going, what they will do when they get there.

The images which result from the responses to these questions will assist students to round out the given circumstances of their roles. The idea of character objectives is being introduced when they must decide what their characters *want* in the improvisation they are about to perform.

This process is repeated throughout the various ages such as 12-18-30-45-60-80. During each stage, the students are asked to freeze, and each in turn to complete a sentence commencing with, "I wish..."

Articulating this wish helps students to become aware of their characters' inner impulses and desires at different life stages; it is aimed to develop insight into already-experienced life stages as well as those not yet experienced, and to steer them away from stereotypical images and superficial acting.

Following this trans-generational sequence they are asked to lie down, close their eyes, and recall their lives-their childhood, their families- and then to focus on one significant event, either happy or sad, which occurred in their childhood. Once more they are fed sensory stimuli to help them recall the sensations surrounding the incident.

To establish immediacy in their descriptions of the event, they are asked to begin the 'poetic sentences' with 'My name is _____. I am _____years old.' Once again, the 'poems' that emerge are integrated with others and become the performance texts.

Student Responses

Students are constantly impressed by the expressive writing that results from the preparation exercises and from the combining of students' works. They also laud the variety of perspectives and staging techniques that evolve out of these drama/writing improvisations. A student wrote:

> This exercise has exposed what I consider to be one very interesting characteristic about our class-the heterogeneity of our viewpoints and, consequently, the variety of performance styles. This is exciting as it gives us a rare opportunity to explore the realm of theatre through so many different perspectives.

Students also comment on how drama enhances their awareness.

> A comment Rebecca made in class strikes me as the most important thing that happened in drama today. She met a blind guy in the grocery store, and he asked her to help him load his knapsack. Before we had done this work in class, she admitted, she would have helped but felt acutely uncomfortable. Now, because she had confronted how she would feel if she were blind herself, she was empathetic to his position. Muriel congratulated her on discovering something important; that the actor's process can affect, and enrich, your entire life.

A variety of preparatory exercises can be found in such books as those listed in Chapter One. The exercises can be used as described, or they may be extended, or adapted to suit your particular group's needs.

Fictional Families

Because I generally begin the fictional family scenes with visualization and physicalization exercises, I often incorporate writing as a follow up to the exercises. The following is an example of how students are helped to create text arising from these exercises.

Step 1: WARM UPS a) Visualization

'Find a comfortable space on the floor. Lie down. Close your eyes. Breathe deeply through your diaphragm. Inhale and exhale. Listen to the sounds of your own breathing. Listen to the sounds of other people's breathing. Listen to the sounds inside the room…and to the sounds outside the room.

As your fictional family character, think back to when you were young. And you played outside on sunny days…and on rainy days. Imagine you are a child playing in a warm rain-shower. Feel the rain on your face and on your body. It is washing away all the tension. Let the water run down on your head, your face, shoulders, neck, chest, back, legs, feet. Enjoy the sensation.'

Step 2: b) Physicalization

'When you feel ready, get up and have fun splashing in the puddles.'

Relaxation exercises lead into sensory experiences including listening, recalling of images and sensations, and active imagining. Movement in character, introduction of appropriate activities (in this case becoming children splashing in puddles) can provide the inspiration for novel and fresh approaches like the poem that Michael wrote which follows.

did you ever wish there were real-live time machines

the kind that have glimmering knobs
and luminous switches
and magical beams
the kind that could take you back
back to the days
when time didn't matter
and peanut brittle did
when teddy bears ruled the world
and Fisher-Price knights rode forth
on rocking horses
and puddles were oceans...

Warm-ups that transform adults into children have an energizing and spontaneous effect on the participants. In this 'puddle' exercise, they splash in the rain, play interactive games and are encouraged to have FUN.

Group Dynamics and the Teacher's Role

Group dynamics vary somewhat in such exercises. This variation has been obvious to me, since I have often taught two consecutive classes of students in the same age group. Frequently, when I have introduced this warm-up, one class might react immediately in a boisterously interactive way, whereas the students in another class might warm up slowly, playing individually at first, miming their games, and eventually building toward interactive verbal activities.

In the past, when I asked one group of fictional family characters to 'return home from their play on the street', they responded immediately like obedient children. A second class, however, yelled and screamed such phrases as "No, we don't want to come in-we're having too much fun-you can't make us." Only my threat as 'parent figure'- "you must come in now, or you'll be punished" influenced them sufficiently to return to their 'homes' and their 'beds'.

It is wise, therefore, not to expect all groups to respond in similar manner. The teacher can always accelerate, or slacken, for that matter, the interactive process by intervention or what Spolin calls 'side coaching' (1960). This type of approach can be used in every exercise. It is especially useful when students have difficulty focusing on their particular activity.

Step 3. Fictional Family Character Preparation

'Find a comfortable space on the floor. Close your eyes. Inhale and exhale deeply. Haaaa, Yaaaa, Laaaa, Maaaa, Mmmmm.

Think about your own childhood- of an event or an incident that you wished could have been different-either because of the way you reacted to it-or because one of your family members did not react in the way you would have wished. Recall the exact circumstances-the sounds, smells, colors, textures.

Now think about your fictional family character's past, and recall an incident when you wished you or your fictional family member would have responded differently.

This incident may have been a turning point in your life. It may have altered your perceptions, your attitudes, your motivations and behaviour. Recall the circumstances in every detail.'

Step 4: Creative Writing

'Sit up, get paper and pencil, and describe the incident in a few poetic sentences.'

(Objectives: To inspire actors to 'live' a significant event in their characters' past. To use drama as a stimulus for creative writing. The students' writings become their original scripts for their performance pieces.)

Step 5: Reading

'Join the circle on the floor, and read your written work aloud to the group.'

Step 6: Assignment

(For next class) prepare a performance piece from your creative piece. If you wish, you may pair up with someone else whose work may contain some similar element to yours.

Step 7: Performance

My Fictional Family Character: A Past Incident

a) Basic Relaxation Exercise

b) 'Move around the room. Warm up your vocal chords. Haaaaaaa, yaaaaaaaa, laaaaaaaa, maaaaaaaa, mmmmmmm. Begin to move as your fictional family character would at the age s/he is in your performance pieces. Go about your character's daily activities. When you have completed your daily activities, sit down ready for the performances to take place.'

A myriad of styles and topics are demonstrated in the various performances. For example, a fictional family character playing a stepmother called Claudia, unpopular with her stepdaughter, expresses her past loneliness:

> My name is Claudia.
> I'm thirteen years old
> Who cares for me?
> Mom-Look at me!
> Talk to me-Dad!
> I'm alone.
>
> I need you! I need to touch you, to hear your voice!
> I need to know you care for me!
>
> Look! Mom-Dad-The sun is shining! Birds are singing.
>
> It's Sunday today!

Let's go out and walk in the park
together as a family,
as a mother, a father and a child!
Please!

And she continues the exercise in her journal:

> This afternoon my character recalled a sad moment of
> her adolescence. This period of her life was difficult
> because she didn't have any communication with her
> parents. They didn't pay much attention to her.
>
> Why? Even today she doesn't understand. She
> knows that her mother had a lot of work to do with her
> four sons. But that's not a reason to be neglectful of a
> daughter, to forget her presence. Claudia needed her
> father and her mother as much as her four little brothers.
> Maybe even more!
>
> When she was a teenager, Claudia felt she was no
> more a member of the family; sometimes she thought
> that she was a stranger to her parents.
>
> 'Mom, look at me! Talk to me Dad!' But no
> answers-a dreadful silence between her parents and her.
> She needed to talk; but there was nobody to listen to
> her. Sometimes she needed to weep bitterly; but there
> was nobody to comfort her. She was alone-alone with
> her tears, her frustration, her fears. She was alone in the
> darkness of her adolescence!
>
> Where is the light? Where is happiness? Who is
> going to show her what is happiness?

In this improvisation Claudia called for help. But she knew that the only
rescuers she needed were her parents. For her it was the last attempt to
catch their attention and their love. After that, it would be too late.

At the end of the improvisation she knew that her parents wouldn't come to her. And she knew that they didn't care for her. But she wasn't able to hate them and she never had the courage to tell her parents that they considered their daughter a stranger. No, it was too late to change this artificial relationship between them.

Step 8. Playwriting

The Fictional Family Ten Years Ago: group (from students' original scripts or outlines.)

> Inventing biographical scenarios to develop character is valuable not only for actors but also for writers of fiction such as novelists, playwrights and screenwriters. The moment a character is born, its interior life begins. As the story unfolds, the exterior life of the character develops. The interaction between the character and its environment, the obstacles it encounters, and its behaviour and responses to that environment and obstacles, reveal the character's personality. (Field, 1982)

Until now, the students, for the most part, were improvising their scenes or writing individually. Now each fictional family is asked to collaborate either on a script, or an outline for a script, to present in class.

(Objectives: To make history an experienced reality in order to elucidate the present situation. To live a past event together with the members of their fictional families. To provide students with an opportunity to collaborate in script development and playwriting.)

A student wrote:

> It was exciting to see how quickly the scenarios were born. Everybody was well enough acquainted with their

characters to immediately decide where they were ten years ago and how they felt at that time.

Step 9: Fictional Family Character's Dream or Nightmare: Group

> The notion of the unconscious is at the heart of the aesthetic experience. The maker of art...is one who gives form to a feeling state. That form, expressed through movement, sound, or visual imagery, embodies a symbolic representation of the unconscious. (Landy, 1986)

(Objectives: To provoke, from the students, imaginative, innovative, often surrealistic depictions of their fictional family character's inner life.

To assist them to express their fictional family characters' unconscious state through theatrical imagery. To inspire them to write imaginatively about the experience.)

I. Warm Up: Mask Movement-Expression

I generally do mask work with students as warm-ups before initiating the dream scenarios. Working with masks immediately preceding the introduction of the FF characters' dreams can suggest the idea of incorporating masks into their performances. The often illogical, fragmented, surreal nature of dreams adapts itself to the abstract, representational quality of masks. In addition, the covering of the face with a mask can release inhibitions, free the body and allow it to move in more flexible, innovative ways.

'I will call out some statements. Act immediately without reflection. Refine your movement. Use your whole body. Define a beginning, middle and end. Make a physical statement. Aim for clarity and economy. First, respond instinctively and make a statement as yourself. Next respond instinctively and make a statement as your FF character.'

Examples: 'I want to fly. I want to play ball. I want to climb the mountain.'

'I will now call out some more statements, adding an obstacle.'

Examples: 'I want to fly but I have no wings. I want to float like a balloon. I want to float like a balloon but I am too heavy. I want to jump over the moon. I want to jump over the moon but my legs are too short.'

At another time I might add a third statement: 'Find a solution.'

II. Character Preparation

'Find a comfortable space on the floor. Lie down. Inhale, exhale through your diaphragm. Haaaaa Yaaaaaa Laaaa Maaaaa Mmmmmm.

Become your fictional family character. Go to sleep and dream your fictional character's dream.

Join your family. Relate your dream. The family will select one dream to perform, or if you wish you may incorporate aspects of other members' dreams as well.'

III. Performance

IV. 'Write about the experience'. **A student wrote:**

> It was a long time ago
> I have almost forgotten my dream.
> But it was there then,
> In front of me
> Bright as the sun-
> My dream.
>
> And then the wall rose
> Rose slowly
> Slowly
> Between me and my dream.
> Rose slowly, slowly
> Dimming

Hiding
The light of my dream
Rose until it touched the sky
The wall.

Shadow
I am black.

I lie down in the shadow
No longer the light of my dream before me,
Above me.
Only the thick wall.
Only the shadow.
My hands!
My dark hands!
Break through the wall.
Find my dream!
Help me to shatter this darkness,
To smash this night,
To break this shadow
Into a thousand lights of sun,
Into a thousand whirling dreams of sun!

And she explained in her journal:

The 'dream' is the objective of the Black actor, the 'wall'
is the accumulation of negative Black stereotypes that
the Black actor must overcome, the 'darkness' represents
the ignorance of Whites toward Black, and the 'sun'
is the new enlightenment of the White audience. A
fulfilment of the 'dream'!

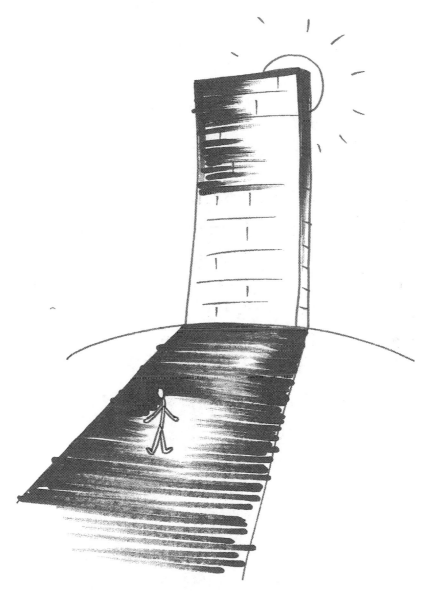

The Wall

Another student wrote:

> When I talked to my family this morning, something strange happened. We all had the same nightmare… We were all in some kind of mystical play in which the landscape was a silvery metallic death. And we had all slowly risen out of this (our) grave, and remembered chasing people for food, frothing at the mouth as we ran across this desert.
>
> And the funny thing was that it was a backward movie in which the ending was people running, and ended with everything clean. Yet it felt like there were no answers left to find. No middle, no centre, and no time. It was chaotic.
>
> We all had the same nightmare, yet it was pure and personal for me. Like a piece of fiction, it came and went like it was nothing-a fleeting glance at my insides-and it was all over.
>
> It was indeed POWERFUL!!!

Secondary Roles

Since many fictional families are 'stepfamilies', some members did not know their present families ten years ago. In these cases, it is suggested that they select other class members to represent the characters they require for their scenes. This gives the selected students an opportunity to play additional roles and also provides the student casting them with directing experience. Playing additional roles is not confined to scenes in the past. Secondary characters are often introduced in improvisations giving all students, from time to time, the opportunity to 'fill in'. Sometimes a fictional family character is resurrected for a particular past event as a student explains here.

It was an interesting experience for Claudia to play a scene in the past with her parents. I know how my family characters are, because I described them in my December journal. So it was easier to explain to Kim and Shawn the kind of parents I needed for the improvisation...their attitude toward my character was exactly what I was expecting: a mother who seemed interested in my life; but she was only asking questions without listening to my answers about what I was doing, how I was feeling.

Kim playing Claudia's mother:

> Today I got to play a ditz, and I loved every minute. I was Claudia's mother when Claudia was an industrious college student plagued by incoherent parents. Her father (played by Shawn) was downright insensitive and apathetic, but the way I played the mother, she was even worse. She would ask the right questions, then get preoccupied and leave the room before the answers, total camp. A blast.

And the scene inspired her to write this monologue.

> Henry, if I could change the past I would
> But it really wasn't my fault
> It all started when you told me to try to be presentable
> You know I hate when you tell me what to do.
> Of course I was indignant and walked away from you,
> And tripped on the carpet,
> and then spilt my clam juice on Mila's gorgeous white satin dress, was it?, dress,
> Which looked so ridiculously funny, if you think about it,

I couldn't help but break out into hysterics
And while I was getting up off the floor
I knocked the punch bowl over,
And then you had to lead me home,
Really, it wasn't my fault.
If you would have just kept quiet and not have told me
what to do
Everything would have been just fine.

Scenes in the past give the fictional family members an opportunity to enact specific fictional family events. Each event adds further dimensions to the lives of the characters. There is no limit to how many of these scenes can be played. Although I suggest that this scene take place ten years ago, this is, of course, flexible. Often students prefer to present scenes which took place eight years ago or twelve years ago, because they feel that particular incidents could only have occurred in that chosen time frame.

Students also initiate their own scenes when they feel there may be issues in their fictional characters' lives which remain unresolved, or because they wish to share with the audience, or outside fictional families, an important family event. They may decide to perform these past scenes as a family group, or more often, their presentations include just one or two other fictional family members. The more scenes they play, the more insights acquired, contributing to the richness of their characters and hence their writing.

Step 10. Post-Performance Discussion
Immediately following performance, I often ask the actors to remain 'on stage' *in character* while we, the audience, ask them questions about the scene they just enacted. These questions generally involve interactions and behaviour with their fictional families. Next, I ask them to 'de-role' and, as actors, they are asked questions pertaining to the theatrical

elements in the scene. They are also asked to articulate any insights gained from their experience either as characters or as actors in the role. And the members of the audience state their observations. Subsequent reflections are noted in students' journals.

Journals

In Chapter One I mentioned that students keep journals to record their experiential process during the period of the course. Excerpts from their journals have also been provided in this chapter. The students also keep **character diaries,** *i.e.*, diaries written in the first person by their fictional family characters. Their journals include all written assignments such as poems, stories, scripts and research material. Students are advised that they may write these journals in any style they wish.

Some students supplement their journals with poems, scripts, drawings and other diary material not directly related to course material. Journal writing is a course requirement to meet the following objectives:

a) to encourage students to reflect on their classroom experiences in order to discourage superficial approaches to their work,

b) to develop an additional means of communication and mutual feedback between me and my students,

c) to provide students with ample opportunity to analyze and evaluate their peers' performances and participation,

d) to validate journal writing as a developmental component of the actor's process.

e) to provide students with an additional opportunity to hone their writing skills

Each of the above objectives is supported by its own rationale.

a) Journal writing to express personal reflections toward academic or practical work is an accepted practice in a variety of disciplines. For example, Pam Barrager Dunne, drama therapist, states that"Writing helps to focus thoughts and to explore feelings. The journal serves as a valuable resource..." (1990, 31). Similarly, Toby Fulwiler, writing professor, states that "The journal is a natural format for self-examination...Journals are interdisciplinary and developmental by nature" (1980, 19).

b) In a class of more than 20 students and a limited time slot, individual feedback and class discussion are often cut short. Also, as mentioned in Chapter One, students who may have been inhibited in group exchange are unexpectedly forthcoming in personal writing. Their candidness helps me to get to know them more quickly and to give feedback in a private, personal way.

c) An important aspect of journal writing is peer evaluation. Peer evaluation is an important component in actor training. Many educators and actor-training theorists stress the value of peer evaluation. For example, Viola Spolin (1963) states:

> ...it is most essential that the teacher-director does not make the evaluation himself [*sic*] but, rather, asks the questions which all answer-including the teacher...Thus audience responsibility for the actors becomes part of the organic growth of the student" (27).

The journals allow for augmentation of class discussions. Although some time is allotted for peer evaluation in class, there is not always sufficient time to hear every student's comments. Second, some students are inhibited in groups. Third, many students are reluctant to evaluate others because they are concerned that their comments may be perceived to be negative. In journal writing, students can openly evaluate their peers because they know that the journal is confidential. I am the only one who reads their comments.

Grading journals is a controversial issue in academic courses. Some teachers feel that journals are personal and should not even be read by teachers. Fulwiler disagrees, and offers the following argument.

> First, a reading by a teacher can help them expand their journals and make them more useful. Second, some students believe that if an academic production is not looked at by teachers it has no worth. Third, students feel that journals must 'count for something'- as must every requirement in an academic setting. (Fulwiler, 1980, 18).

Fulwiler further endorses student journal writing for the benefit of teachers' learning. He states:

Reading students' journals keeps teachers in touch with student frustrations, anxieties, problems, joys, excitements. Teachers, regardless of discipline, who understand the everyday realities of student life may be better teachers when they tailor assignments more precisely toward student needs. Reading student journals humanizes teachers. (18).

Autobiographies

As described in Chapter One, before any scenes are enacted, students write autobiographies for their characters. To help them with this assignment I hand out the following questions.

What was my childhood like?
What were my parents like?
What were my friends like?
Who were my parents?
Who were my grandparents?
Do I feel lonely?

Am I a social person?

What are my ambitions?

What is my state of health?

Whom do I like? Whom do I dislike?

What sorts of people do I like or dislike?

What do I like about myself?

What do I dislike about myself?

What makes me sad?

What makes me happy?

What is my physique?

How do I think other people view me?

How does this differ from the view I have of myself?

How do I deal with conflict?

What is my centre i.e. the most sensitive, expressive part of my body?

With which part of my body do I lead when I move?

What physical and vocal mannerisms do I have?

Who in my fictional family had the greatest influence on my life?

Students continue to add to their autobiographies as they discover, through improvisations and scene work, additional dimensions to their fictional family characters throughout the year. Those students who have had difficulty writing creatively in the past find it surprisingly easy and exciting to write about a character which they themselves have created.

Inner Monologues

In the fictional family technique, inner monologues were initially employed immediately following the crisis scene (see Chapter One). However, when I observed that this device served not only to facilitate actors to probe more deeply their fictional family characters' needs, but also that their delivery helped their fictional family members to gain understanding of those needs, and that this understanding generally resulted in more profound group interaction, gradually I began to use the monologues as interventions during enactment of scenes in which actors seemed unable to express their characters' inner thoughts and/or feelings.

Sometimes students (particularly secondary) will adopt a superficial approach to their roles based on their experience of watching television situation comedies. I never reproach them for their choices or for the ways their characters might behave on stage. Instead, I ask them to freeze and to each deliver a monologue expressing their characters' inner thoughts. This invariably calms down both the actors and audience as they all *listen* carefully to what the character is saying. When the actors discover that they receive much more positive feedback from their work when it is approached maturely, they adopt a more serious approach. By this I do not mean that they cannot perform comedy. Not at all. But they learn that characters have to be real, even in comedy.

Writing the Inner Monologue

Some theatre practitioners use the inner monologue as a rehearsal technique. Moore (1985) directs her actors to write their inner monologues before coming to scene study class and to articulate them before saying their characters' lines from the play. In the fictional family methodology I ask students to include their fictional family characters' inner monologues (both preceding scenes and subsequent to presentation) in their journals.

Benedetti (1981) suggests actors perform their scenes twice, first speaking the inner monologue as though it were the actual text; second, thinking it while articulating the text.

The interior monologue device is a useful way of checking yourself to insure that you have traced the continual line of your character's thought throughout a scene and of being sure that you <u>relive</u> this thinking <u>every time</u> you perform the scene. (87).

Sternberg and Garcia (1989) remind us that soliloquy is a theatre technique which was adapted for socio-drama by Jacob Moreno. Socio-drama directors use it as an intervention technique when a participant is viewed as "stuck", "not in touch with his feelings" or not totally absorbed in the action. The action is stopped and the participant is asked to "soliloquize about what he thinks and feels about the situation." (63).

Shurtleff (1978) stresses the importance of actors' discoveries in their theatre work.

> Acting is a whole series of discoveries. The discoveries
> may be about the other character, or about oneself, or
> about someone who is offstage, or about the situation
> now or the situation as it existed ten years ago and how
> that affects the now. The more discoveries you make in
> a scene, the more interesting your scene will be. (58).

The above quotes can easily be applied to fostering creativity in writing.

Closing Ritual

At the end of the course I initiate a ritual to give closure to the fictional family experience. I will ask each student to write about which characteristics of their character they would like to keep, and which characteristics they would like to discard. Then I ask them to write about what they are taking away from the experience. A student wrote:

> Broken, our family
> Is parted; and the class,
> Too, must go its separate ways.
> Everyone has gained and given,
> Many have changed forever.

In the end, everyone benefits from everyone, and
None of us goes away empty.
Even apart, we are family.

Summary

This chapter has illustrated the FF dramatic technique's use in the development of writing skills, in creative writing (playwriting, poetry), journals, free-flow inner monologues and integration of individual work to create performance pieces. It has offered examples of my students' writing inspired by the stimuli of the FF's use of visualization, physicalization and improvisational exercises.

A former student of mine who uses the FF methodology in her secondary school drama classes sent me her assessment of the work's influence on her students. The following is just one example of her assessments. (Student's name has been changed.)

> John Brown's work, although a bit twisted, is a great example of how well this project works for students with severe problems. He is sixteen years old, is repeating Section II for the third time and has never, in his High School career, handed in such an extensive piece of work. His character autobiography consists of five neatly typed pages. He is a drug user, has been in juvenile court and comes from a broken home. I am extremely pleased with his progress, self-discipline and control since he has begun the fictional family.

References

Appel, Libby. *Mask Characterization: An Acting Process.* Carbondale. Southern Illinois University Press, 1982

Benedetti, Robert: *The Actor at Work.* Englewood Cliffs, N.J. Prentice Hall, 1970.

Dunne, Pamela Darranger. *The Creative Therapeutic Thinker.* Encino, Ca. Center for Psychological Change, 1990.

Field, Syd. *Screenplay: The Foundations of Screenwriting.* New York. Dell Publishing, 1982.

Fulwiler, Toby. "Journals across the Disciplines." Urbana, Ill. *English Journal,* National Council of Teachers of English, Vol. 69, No. 9, pps 14-19, Dec., 1980.

Gold, Muriel. *The Fictional Family In Drama, Education and Groupwork.* Springfield, Ill. Charles C Thomas, 1991.

Landy, Robert. *Drama Therapy: concepts and practices.* Springfield, Ill. Charles C Thomas, 1985

Moore, Sonia. *The Stanislavski System.* New York. Penguin. 1984.

Moore, Sonia. *Training an Actor.* New York. Penguin, 1985.

Shurtleff, Michael. *Audition.* New York. Walker & Co.,1978

Spolin, Viola: *Improvisation for the Theatre.* Evanston, Ill.

Northwestern University Press, 1960.

Stanislavski, Constantin. *Creating a Role.* New York. Theatre Arts, 1961

Sternberg and Garcia. *Sociodrama: Who's In Your Shoes?* New York. Praeger, 1989

Way, Brian. *Development Through Drama.* London. Longman, 1967

Chapter Five:

Acting as Inspiration for Poetry

Michael Sommers

Ever since I was quite young, I have always been very compelled by both writing and acting. Through these creative media of communication, I have seen, felt, and experienced an astounding diversity of images, feelings, impressions, emotions, people, worlds...with whom I would never otherwise have come into contact. Through drama and poetry, I have stretched my mind. I have entered scenes more life-like than reality. I have wandered through verses more imaginary than my wildest fictions. Through poetry and drama, I have even flown to the moon. And that is kind of what life is about-At least once in a while-Flying to the moon.

In the past, I have written poetry on and off, but I had done little acting since I was in public school. This class (Fundamentals of Drama) offered me the unexpected opportunity to combine the two activities-and the results were very rewarding. I became increasingly aware of how much interdependence exists between writing and acting. Acting could inspire what I write. After reading two books that discuss methods of teaching poetry to children (ones that I found very similar to many techniques used in this Drama class) this link between the two forms of expression became concrete.

There are countless fundamental similarities between poetry and drama. Both require imagination, experimentation, and rigorous attention to precise detail. Both are imitations of life, attempting to create more vivid, colourfully interpreted landscapes. They both give creative expression to themes, issues, conflicts, and situations that occur in the world, and at the same time, offer their own solutions to them while also (and very importantly) strive to entertain, to stir, and to move their audiences by taking into account all of the human senses and their reactions.

Because, in fact there are so many creative links between drama and poetry, it is not at all surprising that when "both drama and written expression (are employed together) a double benefit should result" (Powell, 1968, p. 87). This was the case for me personally. Faced with the task of describing and commenting upon the many exercises I had completed in class, I was not, at first, feeling overly enthusiastic about going home twice a week to scribble dry and lifeless notes into a "Journal". Nor was I bursting with passion to be given another "Dear Diary" project, with the expected first person confessions slotted into nice, little grammatically correct paragraphs. I think, in retrospect, that I rather underestimated my teacher, Muriel Gold.

Right from the beginning, Muriel was very clear in emphasizing the fact that these journals were OURS. We could write anything in them that we wanted, in any way that we wanted-as any person we wanted to be, in any language we wanted to speak, in any color we wanted to write (it had to be legible of course). No grammar, no rules, no order, no logic...in short...FREEDOM.

I was free to let my imagination run wild-to write whatever I wanted, and more importantly, I could write however I wanted. Immediately my Journal lost any claims it ever had to being a mere "assignment" (Koch, 1970, p.3) and became an imaginative outlet, a creation. "Encouraging children to be free and even 'crazy' in what they wr(i)te...ha(s) especially good results. They wr(i)te freely and crazily and they (like) what they (are) doing because they (are) writing beautiful and vivid things" (Ibid, p 17). Because I felt this lack of constraint I was able to experiment a lot with my Journal. I found that my "writing quickly became richer and more colourful" (Ibid, p.10).

> hang loose loose loose
>> rag doll swaying on crazy carpet
>
> bounce bounce seaweed and waves
>> mind going wild, mind going free
>> shakin' out my mind on the crazy carpet
>
> shake shake shake

This excerpt from my September Journal reflects the new sense of freedom I had in writing. Not stopping to capitalize the letters or punctuate the lines, I was able to create a very instinctive, spontaneous flow of words that really captured the spirit of free movement that I had experienced when "shaking out".

The fact that this movement I have just described was free, is very significant. For not only did Muriel, from the outset, insist upon freedom in our Journals, she also stressed a great amount of freedom in our acting exercises, particularly the early ones. "The role of the teacher should be that of a guide who presents suggestions which will enable every pupil to discover inspiration and new meaning for himself." (Powell, op. cit., p. 36).

Muriel guided us and gave us ideas-but, what was ultimately performed, was created by us-the actors. We were expected to stretch our imaginations, expand our sense, bring past experiences into play. We were not criticized or constrained by techniques. Never were we told precisely what we should act and how we should act it. Muriel exposed us to ideas-ideas that inspired acting, and, after being dramatized, inspired the poetry of my Journal. "I do not mean to say the idea wrote the poems: (I) did. The idea helped (me) to find that (I) could do it, by (giving me) something to write about which really interested (me)" (Koch, op. cit., p.5).

What made the scenes and improvisations we acted out, and the poems I ultimately wrote, as original and diverse as they were, was the enormous variety of methods that Muriel used, to inspire us. Once the idea had been introduced to us, it took root in our minds, and using imagination and instinct, we would act it out. Perform it. Become it.

Sometimes, this idea was an "activity" (Powell, op. cit.) like playing in the rain puddles after a storm as a child. I would imagine the puddles, imagine the wet, create an image of the situation in my mind, and react to it, joyfully, letting loose in silence my pleasure in puddle dancing. I was concentrating on enjoying myself in those puddles, by myself and with others. The activity inspired the movements, the gestures, the attitude, and the fictional family character. It then inspired the poem in my November Journal:

> whatever happened to puddles
> deep pools of innocence
> soft pools of mud
> squishy, soggy, cold, rippled
> i can make islands in the puddles
> I'm a little yellow god
> black splatters up my pants
> sidewalk spray down my socks
> i laughed so hard
> after the rain
> i prayed for the storm
> wished for the torrent
> and danced in my yellow christopher robin boots
> i splashed all the girls
> and i smooshed all the worms
> and i laughed so hard

they don't make laughs like that any more
puddle laughs

Like the activity itself, the poem is very dynamic. Its verbs: "laugh", "spray", "splatters", "danced", "wished", "smooshed", are all key movements in my personal, acted-out, experience of puddle dancing. Movement, a central part of acting, is thus also an integral aspect of poetry. Just as movement defines a dramatic character, distinguishing his/her attitudes and imbuing him/her with personality and life, so does movement define poetry; reflecting a mood, creating a rhythm and speed, that gives a poem its identity and shape its impact.

The motions of a character reveal a lot about that character's identity. In playing Snake Jordan, the character in my fictional family, I spend a lot of time concentrating on the way he moves. He moves slowly and he slouches-and that reflects his laziness, his irresponsibility, and also his generally relaxed attitude towards life. He carries his head up high, with his jaw thrust out a little- and this complements his often defiant and defensive personality. In class, we focus a great deal on our characters' movement. Muriel does not tell us how to move- that decision is left to us. But she gives us the idea to move. A walk says a lot:

I'm walking around the room like Snake wow that
Snake is such a slouchy grouchy guy why doesn't
he take his hands out of his pockets why
does he slide around like a lazy ghost without
chains he ain't got a lilt to his walk oh boy
not only an attitude problem but a posture problem
too slither slap slide slow slink slash slurp
slick slay slooower slim sloshed slave slip
sloooower slooooooooow down Snake...stop

After doing a walk, I have felt it. And after feeling a walk, I can write about it. We were asked to walk as ourselves then transform our movement into our fictional family character's rhythm and movement.

> walk around the room as me
> stride around as Snake
> which one is the real me?
> which one is the fake?
> shifting into one walk
> and slide out of a trance
> when Snake he walks it's lazy struts
> when me, I walk, I dance

A person's movements are fairly conventional, however. To move like one imagines an inanimate object would, requires much more of an imaginative stretch. Muriel often inspired us to move as if we were different inanimate objects: clocks, candles, sculptures. In moving as we imagined these objects would, we were acting like them. In acting like them we became them.

"The exercise is intended principally as a means of letting the pupil experience a subject from the inside, hence making it more realistic." (Powell, op. cit., p. 48).

Not only does this technique help inspire one's acting, it also can greatly enhance one's poetry. "(One) is likely to write more enthusiastically and more imaginatively…(if one) feels for the subjects rather than merely observe them."… "The lasting value of this exercise is that the pupil, once having become involved in any subject, can use this experience to imagine any number of additional situations at any time in the future. Although he may never have tried being a snake slithering through the grass, if he is asked to write a poem or a piece of prose on the snake, his imagination should enable him to do so…He can thus create an atmosphere of realism for himself, and hence write from the inside out" (Powell, op. cit., p.49).

candle
- strong and tall and straight and chanukah
refined and ornate, sunk into a chandelier
cake, sticky feet plastered in the sprinkles
and mud and sugar and fireworks and tiny
silver beads that are tears from the columbia
pictures lady
- christmas and angels and the sweet old
statue of liberty with the green light
at the end of the dock and daisy and gatsby
and jazz in love when they smile across
the sea and tremble, so don't shoot me into
the swimming pool.

candle
light me
and I melt
and swirl, trickle, drip, roll, slide, slither,
writhe, wither, collapse, lean, sigh, spread,
spread, spread, spread

dead wax
on the floor

In this poem, from my October Journal, I was a candle on a birthday cake. I was told to imagine myself as a candle. To feel myself on top of a cake, to hear the sounds and smell the smells around me. And then I was lit. And I was to melt, moving not as a person, but as a stick of burning wax. Both the sensations I experienced and the associations that my mind connected with my actions emerged in this poem. But probably the most vivid are the sensations.

This exercise led into a scene in Snake's past when he was ten years old and he would be meeting a character his age from one of the other fictional families (Gold, 1991).

> think Snake
> at ten
> walk Snake
> at ten
> kind of an Oliver
> kind of another identity
> a slouch and a half on rye
> please, please, pay attention to me
> love me, love me, love me
> I dare you
> to follow me
> to do
> anything I can do
> which is everything
> from Antarctica to Alaska
> and back
> in the sky
> I dare you
> I even kind of want to scare you
> and if I met another character
> from another family
> it might be Matthew
> and there might be conflict
> we'd want different things
> I'd want the moon
> and he'd want to watch me take it

without burning himself
well, I'd get burnt
'cause that's what youth is for
getting burnt
but under the burn
the ashes and embers and mad sad charcoal rust
I'd still really only
want to be loved
another dimension
to all this attention
and I think to myself
intention
intention
well isn't that the key
to acting...
what makes drama dramatic is conflict between characters

Before acting out our fictional family scenes we were often asked to visualize our own families to stimulate our sense memory of an environment analogous to the one we might create in our scene (Gold, 1991). A breakfast scene inspired the following verse.

Family Time
Thinkin' about my family
my real family
the one in Toronto
and how we have breakfast
together
(which never happens)
'cause my mama
sleeps in 'til
real late

Scarlette O'Hara
up in bed
third floor tower
takin' an hour shower
makes it down
for eleven instead
and then my daddy
wakes up at the crack
o'dawn
a pioneer man
on the fresh-hatched street
he walks all round
towin' the shadows
of his feet
and then my sis
sleeps somethin' fierce
her rebel radio
just can't pierce
her pillowed ears
she switches gears
and flies to school
as nine appears
and I'm a crank
fell out o'bed
and hit the wrong side
of my head
can't stand the lights
can't stand the sounds
I make the kitchen
out of bounds

All forms of artistic expression depend heavily upon sensual experience, but perhaps none so acutely as do both drama and poetry. Both acting and writing have as their purpose the revelation of life in all of its subjective and intricate detail. In acting every specific movement, gesture, look, and utterance conveys meaning, just as in poetry, every precise word, image, sound, and structure contains significance. Yet, in both cases, the ideas behind these results are inspired by the senses.

Many of the acting exercises we did in class, focused upon the exploration of the senses-experiencing blindness, pretending to be without hearing, touch, smell, listening to certain sounds. Through these experiences, we became more aware of our bodies and our perceptions, and indirectly I was given many new sources for writing my Journals. Experiencing blindness was a very rich experience for me-both as an actor and a writer. After being blindfolded for a while, I felt confused and lost-my hearing and sense of touch both seemed to sharpen. Without the distraction of sight, I was able to concentrate on these more subtle sense perceptions:

And blindness starts secure like last sun
rays into the forest
And then black foresty dusky forever night
Forever stumble tunnel of carousel walls
Labyrinth, then more sure-the tread
'til obstacles-mirage walls and people
explosions out of nowhere
We all have hands
And no eyes
Climbing a mountain in the dark
Midnight scaling and dizziness
Small sound to turn me round
I'm out of bounds

Blindness-forever night

In this instance, a lot of my experience was derived through the sense of touch-feeling the details of my surroundings. But another sense that contributed to my acting, and especially to my writing, was that of hearing. "Sound is an important part of poetry." (Koch, *op. cit.,* p. 126) And Muriel often created situations in class that helped me to "associate sounds freely with other things and find enjoyable sound comparisons" (Ibid.) that made my poetry much more imaginative. One exercise was aimed to help us understand Brecht's concept of scenic gestus, which we would then incorporate into our fictional family scenes (Gold, 1991). In my Journal, I wrote about my experience of lying on the floor, eyes

closed, and as Muriel guided us, listening to and concentrating on the
sounds of the breathing around me:

so anyway-we're here breathing and breathing
-in and out-like snores and tides and
vacuum cleaners going backwards-and if we
close our eyes then the sardines in stocking
feet can hear one another breathing and
it sounds very eerie when all of these seventeen
sexy sardine sighs get packed together,
one by one, into a sole and unique big fat
crescendoing monster breath-you crazy old
spectacled scientists are going to go mad-
spill your beakers of sodium cornflakes
all over the moon-have you ever seen seventeen
sexy sighing sardines turn into one big
monster in the space of five minutes?
-methinks no-one big ocean-one big
salmon-one big sigh-I'm so relaxed
numb and fading on my raft of respiration
-let the others carry me along with their
exhalations-I'm falling asleep...

As you can see, the initial sensory experience provides the poetic idea,
and from there the imagination sweeps it away, weaving a multitude
of off-shooting images, sensations, and associations into the context of
the original perception. And the act becomes poetic. And thus, in an
environment that nurtures creativity and freedom, acting, through its
many facets, can inspire poetry

Muriel guides us

-"and I'm joyful"

hey man! I'm joyful and I'm more than joyful, I'm in ecstasy and I'm sailing and striving and smiling enough to bust my face and for some strange reason my sweet, sunny voice singing: "joyful...joyful" has gone up real high-like to reflect my mood and I didn't even do it on purpose and I'm bouncing on the balls of my feet, surrounded by invisible colours and flowers and mountains and moon rays and the people everywhere are exciting me to dance because there are all these wonderful strands of mercury music flooding the space and energy's pounding all over and...

References

Gold, Muriel. *The Fictional Family In Drama, Education, and Groupwork.* Springfield, Ill., Charles C Thomas, 1991

Koch, Kenneth. *Wishes, Lies, and Dreams.* New York. Vintage Books/ Chelsea House Publishers, 1970

Powell, Brian. *English Through Poetry Writing.* London. Heinemann Educational Books Ltd., 1968

Chapter Six:

Teaching History beyond the Lecture Hall
The Uses of the Fictional Family
Model as a Pedagogical Tool within
the History Curriculum

Samuel Kalman

What is the value of a degree in History today? What does it mean, for that matter, to be a university-educated individual today? What tools or skills should an education provide for the student by the time of graduation? These are all questions which must be addressed by the contemporary teacher of History. The problems which they imply are enormous, and the issue of relevancy is perhaps the most pronounced.

Throughout the Humanities, the doctrine of 'publish or perish' is today joined by the question of pedagogical method. For the modern historian teaching at the university level, it is no longer sufficient to simply lecture at the students throughout the course of a term on a variety of prefabricated topics; rather, student needs as we enter the twenty-first century are forcing the adoption of new academic standards, which are in turn producing the need for new approaches to the teaching of history in the classroom.

For those of us in the field of History, the ultimate issue is one of survival. History has traditionally been the target for those who see it as a moribund discipline, bereft of any practical value. More than a century ago, Frederick Wilhelm Nietzsche proclaimed, in his essay on The Use and Abuse of History, that history merely mummifies life, a dead discipline which encourages inaction in the present by concentrating solely on the preservation of useless memories.[1] This "malady of history" could only be cured by a rejection of all traditional historical methodology, placing the emphasis squarely on history as a means to stimulate present action. Post-modernists today have taken this idea one step further, echoing Derrida's theory of 'logocentrism', in arguing that history as it is traditionally practiced is flawed because facts and their interpretation are dependent on the reader or author.[2] Thus not only is the writing of history biased to the point of being worthless, but the reader of the finished product will only further muddle matters by carrying his or her own intellectual baggage into any reading of the final product. Finally, the Historian is increasingly besieged by concepts of 'the end of history'.

Marxist dialectics may no longer be accepted currency in the field of history, but noted scholar Francis Fukuyama has resurrected historical determinism with his concept of 'Universal History'.According to this model, all of human history has been leading up to the victory throughout the world of Liberal Democracy.[3] Hence, why study history at all, one might ask?

This is not merely an academic issue unfortunately, confined to the ivory tower. Politicians continually speak of the value of education, and what, in the era of budget cuts, is to be preserved. Whole departments are being excised at North American universities as a result of such decisions.

Yet when the Canadian and American government ministers and officials talk of the competitiveness of the education systems, and the need to meet modern global standards, they inevitably mention computers and engineering, or science and technology as a whole.[4] The Humanities and History, by contrast, are rarely discussed. Interest, enrolment, and consequently financial resources have dwindled as a result in the past decade, as research grants and departmental resources are whittled down. It would appear that parents and students are listening to what these leaders have to say, and are growing concerned. Although not wishing to over-generalize, the response of historians has been muted at best.[5] In my own field, the current debate is about 'text versus context', focusing on the documents used by the modern researcher.[6] Historians seem to have forgotten the main reason for their employment at the university level: the student.

It is a given that most students enrolled in History programs today at universities across North America will not be going to graduate school. There are few faculty positions available for those who complete a Ph.D., and as governments, both provincial and federal, cut their budgets and civil service rosters to the bone, another option disappears. Most students, therefore, must turn to the world of business to find employment; a company must hire them. All will be required to possess critical thinking skills and the ability to learn and perform a variety of different tasks of various natures, from giving audio-visual presentations to working extensively with computers. Yet at the same time, no department of history wishes to become a mere trade school producing business ready recruits. There is still the need to create the 'educated person'.

Neither of these goals is met today. We continue to rely solely on textbooks and factual information, at the expense of critical thinking and creativity. The pattern is a familiar one: The first three years of a history program are spent memorizing facts which are then regurgitated in the final exams. Essays are written in which the student borrows ideas and information from a number of secondary sources. Finally in their last year the student enters one seminar course, during which he or she gives one or two brief presentations and finally undertakes a project based on original research. Then it is off to the job hunt.

This is, quite simply, the Assembly-Line model of education. We use the same curriculum year in and year out, pushing students through the program and leaving them with few skills, rapidly diminishing prospects, and no real knowledge. In order to succeed as teachers, we must re-examine the way that we as educators and historians go about the business of teaching as we head into the twenty-first century. We must cease to view the classroom as solely textbook- and lecture-based, using rote memorization and exams as the only classroom tools of any practical use.

Studies have shown again and again that most students do not retain information in such an environment. Howard Gardner, in his work on Multiple Intelligence Theory, has demonstrated that some are visual, some are auditory, and some learn more through written exercises.[7] Thus their ability to think critically or to perform certain tasks cannot be adequately gauged through note-taking. How can we therefore move away from this exclusive methodology?

One of the best methods to satisfy all of the above criteria is the Fictional Family model, as proposed by McGill educator Muriel Gold.[8] Although Professor Gold developed this model for use in Drama courses, a reworked Fictional Family is ultimately very useful for the teacher of History at the university level. Using this model allows the instructor to involve all types of learning-auditory, written, and visual. It also forces the student to think critically, rather than merely repeating facts handed out in a textbook or a lecture. The emphasis in this exercise is on a real understanding of history, and its inherent complexity, which the text or lecture often cannot convey.

Obviously, given the evident structural differences between the goals of the history curriculum and those of a Drama or Theatre program, the exercise must be radically modified. Where the Drama instructor and students may have the luxury of an entire semester in which to develop their familial characters and relationships, the history class may have as little as one session's time for completion of the fictional family exercise.

Yet the basic structure of the fictional family model remains the same. Four groups of four to six students (depending on class size) are chosen at random to create a fictional family. The general aim of each group is to give the family both a 'past' and a 'present' setting, according to the period being covered in the class and socioeconomic or political situation during the era in question. They must, in short, give the family a history, based on parameters given out by the instructor.

Thus in a class on the French Revolutionary era, the instructor could assign four families respectively representing the peasantry, the emerging bourgeoisie, the nobility, and church (perhaps a group of priests from the same abbey). The students must adopt a point of view, a distinctive perspective on the events of the day; rather than merely reading about the various doctrinal positions in a textbook, they must now become the characters about which they read, mobilizing the wealth of textbook and lecture material amassed in prior weeks, to create an authentic historical agent.

The students are then asked to prepare the families for presentation and debate in the following class. They must each assume a specific familial role of their own, whose character they will assume during the session. As in Professor Gold's model, all relevant personal data must be created and employed. Details such as family role (father, mother, son, daughter, *etc.*), profession, religion, political views, and economic status are created by each student in consultation with the other fictional family members.[9] A consideration of the actual historical background is crucial during this process.

If using families from the era of Imperialism, what experiences have the families had? Was the family of British gentry stationed in India, for years suppressing the local population? Has the working class German family seen the father join the newly emergent socialist party or a trade union? What is the view of the upper class French wife who is educated, yet sees success only for her husband, whose rich business interests in Africa keep him away much of the time, and leave her feeling angry and suppressed? Issues such as gender, colonialism, and the emergence of organized labour form an important part of the setting in these cases, and are ideal focal points for the created family. There is no shortage of possibilities here.

Yet it is crucial for the instructor to stress both everyday characteristics (the day-to-day life of the family member in question, professions, societal roles), and responsive ones (political views, social mores). Both will naturally differ greatly according to the background of the character and setting at hand, yet both are equally 'historical' and thus should be given equal weight. Only in combining the two will the historical value of the character be fully realized, with the further addition of the character's past.

The family here operates as a logical choice for the enabling of a historical understanding based on actual day-to-day experience. The instructor too often conveys solely the 'Great Man' theory of history, as do textbooks. Thus we teach the Napoleonic era as a series of political events, wars, and legislation. Although such information is vital to a complete understanding of history, they at times overshadow the historical reality on a larger scale. The communist era in the Soviet Union is reduced to the experience of the cold war, at best the rule of ideology as governing principle, whose purges and structural system affected millions of anonymous faces.

Those who lived through these periods, and their experiences at the time, are ignored. Change is too often portrayed only at the official level, involving government, military campaigns, or the great thinkers of the day (the scientific revolution, great philosophers, *etc.*). Even social history is far too often quantitative in nature, at times presenting the genuine daily experiences of the day only in numerical/statistical form.

The fictional family, in contrast to this, is a tool for understanding lived historical reality, encompassing all facets of history-social, political, intellectual, and cultural. By using the family, the instructor is able to allow the students to gain an understanding of lived historical reality.

Furthermore, the family is a unit to which the students themselves can relate, not as far removed from their own experience as the life and times, and the decisions and leadership, of monarchs, generals, and philosophers. The family, as the common social unit in all historical periods, is thus the ideal choice. As Doctor Gold writes:

> The family forms a common basis of experience, a unit to which everyone can relate. Even the most sheltered and naive university students have been exposed all their lives to the depth and intricacy of family relationships. Their perceptions, their communication styles and their modes of interacting have been shaped within the confines of their own families.

This gives the model a much higher chance for success, as some identification with the subject is already present in the students before the creation of the individual characters. In working together on a fictional family project, the individual members thus bring with them a collective experience which can serve as an effective base on which to create their historical characters, but also infuse their family with a real group dynamic, as the project is both individual (the character is one's own creation based on an assigned role), and collective (the interaction of the group members both in the process of family creation and in the acting out of historical reality).

The lecture cannot be completely abandoned as a teaching tool in a history classroom, and therefore time is the key factor limiting the scope of this exercise within a history class. Professor Gold's Drama students sometimes have the luxury of a whole year in which to develop the characters and dynamics of the family. Within the bounds of the history curriculum, however, the fictional family exercise should ideally focus on one session per historical topic.

An allotted time of thirty to thirty-five minutes per week should be sufficient for these purposes. As up to twenty-four students can participate each week if the exercise is used once a week, the size of the class is not a factor, as all students will eventually play a role. If the class is larger, then the various groups will simply be assigned different fictional family topics. An exercise focusing on the Great Depression with one set of students would be followed by one on Nazi Germany with another set of students and so on until all of the students have participated. Thus the fictional family can be utilized in almost any class at any level of study, while the chronological integrity of the curriculum is maintained.

In the event that the class is smaller in size, a third-year seminar for example, the exercise can (and should) be repeated during the course of a term or year. In such situations fewer families may be used. The effective minimum required is nine students, forming three small families.

The maximum of twenty-four reflects four families of six members each. More families, or more students per family unit, becomes too unwieldy, especially during the discussion/debate portion of the activity. Selection of the groups should take place at the end of the introductory class, and be done at random.

The key is to provide a group activity in which the emphasis is on creation as a group. The skills involved should also de-emphasize pre-existing friendships in group selection, instead attempting to gauge the ability of various students to work as a group without previous knowledge of the other group members.

Preparation by the groups must be twofold. Firstly, they must be ready to present the family to the class. Each member must give a brief summary of his or her family member's life history, role in the family and society, and views or attitudes on social, political, cultural, and/or economic issues. This will vary according to period of study and family type; the peasant during the French revolutionary era may have known precious little about cultural and high political issues of the day, but would have had plenty to say regarding economic or social issues and problems at the time. The noble, on the other hand, would probably have had the opposite concerns. This discussion should take no more than twenty minutes. The remaining time can be used by staging a debate between the families. This enables the issues of the day to come out into the open. Arguments and contentious issues of the era can then be re-enacted.

Thus a British liberal bourgeois family and conservative old-moneyed family can debate the home-rule issue with a working-class or Irish farm family, and by extension British-Irish politics and relations throughout the eighteenth and nineteenth centuries can be debated as well. This segment can be run using previously prepared topics (such as the one mentioned above) and questions, but flexibility must be shown, as the exercise is not a scripted one. The students must be allowed the freedom to think for themselves, and to carry the debate in many potential directions. Having read the assigned textbook readings, and heard class lectures, perhaps even that day, on the topic at hand, the students have been given much historical background information on which to draw.

Students who do not directly take part in the fictional family of the week can and should enter the debate by directing previously prepared questions to the families, or by entering the discussion with the families during the latter part of the exercise. The professor in such cases will also act as a moderator, to ensure that all family units are given a fair chance to speak out during the debate, and to allow for a limited number of questions or comments from the remaining students.[1] The primary focus must still be the families themselves, as all will get a chance to eventually participate fully in the exercise by the end of the term/year.

Case #1: A Prototypical Fictional Family History Class-Year One or Two

Basic Setting (Related by instructor to the groups):

May 5, 1789. The date in question is the opening day of the Estates-General in pre-revolutionary France. Pressure is mounting against the monarchy, the result of a mounting financial crisis brought on by overspending and expensive military campaigns under the rule of Louis XIV. Absolutism, as a system of government, is crumbling due to abuse of power, court intrigue, and current King Louis XVI's disinterest in governing the nation. In the midst of the deepening crisis, the King convenes the Estates-General, composed of the clergy (the first estate), the nobility (the second), and the emerging middle-class/common labourers/rural population (the third), to gather and present the Cahiers des Doléances (grievances to the royal government). The four families in this exercise are part of these meetings, which called upon virtually the entire nation to be represented by local delegates.

The Families:

Family 1: A Peasant Family from Provence, poor yet of long standing. They have two children, a son and a daughter. They are poor, yet not starving, but their situation is worsening by the day, as the local noble has raised the rent owed, and prices are falling dramatically. They are uneducated, yet mistrust the nobility.

Family 2: A middle-class Parisian family, part of the emerging bourgeoisie craving political change in France, seeking opportunities to advance further. The father works as a physician servicing the nobility and other members of the middle class, while the mother runs a fashionable salon in the city where writers, thinkers, and musicians gather to discuss the issues of the day. They have two children: one older son in training to work in the emerging merchant concerns of the day, the other a daughter engaged to the owner of a hypothecary.

Family 3: A noble family from Dijon, from the old and wealthy local landowning class. Both the father and the mother grew up in Versailles, at the royal court. They have only one child, a daughter who they are hoping to see married to the son of another old aristocratic family. They see the King as unsuitable to the tasks of the monarchy, yet fear the consequences should he be removed.

Family 4: Not a family in the strict sense, but a group of priests and a cardinal. Two of the priests are from a small rural parish, and one is from Paris. The Cardinal lives at Versailles and ministers to the King. They wish to preserve the status quo of the church as a dominant player in French political and moral life.

All of the students involved will have had a lecture on the French revolutionary era and its aftermath. They will have read the relevant assigned readings on the events, both chapters in the text-book, and primary documents from the period (such as a selection from the *Cahiers de Doléances*).

This critical interaction has two other useful pedagogical consequences: It forces the students to think critically, and also addresses the needs of all types of student-visual, auditory, and writing-based. Critical thinking skills are rarely present in the standard academic routine, which emphasizes rote memory above all. The assembly-line model of education in its historical variant, based exclusively on exams and essays consisting of facts collected from other texts, has little room for intellectual engagement with the subject. Students are thus badly prepared by their university education in a twofold sense.

Firstly, the student is not adequately prepared for life after the university years, for very few potential careers in the non-academic world require rote memory and basic research skills alone as criteria for employment. But perhaps more importantly, the goal of the university, to create a well-rounded and educated graduate, is not accomplished within the current parameters of the curriculum. The fictional family model necessitates critical engagement with the texts provided and, in conjunction with the traditional vehicles of lectures and required readings, mobilizes the creative abilities of the student to a far greater degree.

Furthermore, all learning types can participate in the fictional family exercise with equally beneficial results. The traditional curriculum exclusively emphasizes written and auditory skills. Those students who flourish through auditory comprehension (the lecture) and written exercises (essays, exams), in some way benefit in the process. Yet many others, those who learn visually or verbally, are not even considered. The fictional family is a multi-type exercise, mobilizing verbal skills (the debate/discussion), writing skills (the creation of the character), and auditory skills (the group interaction), and thus allows all students to participate using their type of skills and learning.

The fictional family model can also be modified specifically for a history curriculum. One of the best exercises which keeps the role-playing elements of the fictional family intact, while allowing the class to address a historical situation *en-soi* is the trial of a historical figure.

Although the trial exercise is an old stand-by in the teaching of history, the version presented here is *sui-generis*. The exercise normally focuses solely on the 'Great Men' of history, from witnesses to prosecutors, ignoring genuine historical experience. As described below, the fictional family component removes the emphasis on student/participant repetition of lecture notes and textbook passages, replacing them with critical thinking and a creative recreation of lived history.

This exercise is particularly effective when studying events such as the Russian Revolution or the Paris Commune, with the students each assuming a role in the process of putting a historical figure from such periods on trial. The classroom thus becomes a courtroom, with students acting as the figure on trial, the defence team (no more than three members), the prosecution (no more than three), witnesses (six to eight) and the jury (six to eight). Once again, students involved in this variant must go beyond the mere memorization of facts in a textbook or lecture notes, critically examining a series of historical issues in the process of active engagement as participants in a simulated event. They become a new type of fictional family, a legal one. The instructor acts as the judge, ensuring that order is kept during the proceedings.

There are two methods for the running of this exercise in the classroom. The first would see advance preparation, as with the fictional family model. Students will come to the classroom having met with their groups previously, the prosecution team and the defence team/defendant, and their prospective witnesses. Each will have a prepared case, including opening statements, and a set of questions to ask their witnesses, and for cross-examination. The opening statements should take no more than two to three minutes. The witnesses can then be called, with a maximum of ten minutes allotted for examination and cross-examination. The concluding statements are then read, and the jury is excused for ten minutes, to come to a decision amongst themselves. Finally the verdict is read out, and the trial ends, whereby the instructor can ask or field questions on issues raised during the trial until the class ends. As an alternative, this exercise can also be run entirely within the class itself if time permits, with the instructor allowing a brief fifteen to twenty minutes for each group to prepare.

Case # 2. The Trial: V. I. Lenin. Third Year History Class

The Setting: Russia, after the revolution. Lenin is called upon to defend his actions, as a young revolutionary, later as the leader of the Bolsheviks, and finally as leader of the newly-formed Soviet Union.

The Players:
> The Defendant: V.I. Lenin
> Prosecuting Attorney and 1-2 assistants
> Defense Attorney and 1-2 assistants
> Witnesses for the Prosecution:
> Nicholas Romanov/the last Tsar of Russia
> President Woodrow Wilson
> A member of the Opposition Menshavik Party
> An ex-member of the CHEKA Soviet secret police

> Witnesses for the Defense:
> Leon Trotsky
> Karl Marx
> A non-communist Russian factory worker
> A Western Communist intellectual

> Jury: 6-8 students
> Judge: the instructor

The reader will note the balancing of known historical actors (Lenin, Marx, Wilson), with less familiar characters (factory worker, secret policeman, intellectual). Each fictional participant is also required to create a fictional family, including the jurors and the lawyers involved with the case. These characters should be prepared in writing in advance, and described to the class at the beginning of the trial exercise. This additional component allows a deeper historical understanding of both the issues present at the time, and the motivations of the various historical actors from the man on the street to those in positions of power. Thus the jury may contain rabid supporters of hard-line communism, less rabid party adherents, and anarchists opposed to the state entirely, alongside representatives of pre-revolutionary Russian industry, peasants suspicious of 'urban' communists, and deposed Russian nobles. Similarly, the prosecuting attorneys could be *Menshaviks*-proponents of evolutionary socialism who opposed Lenin-or they could be die-hard American anti-communists.

As with the fictional family, the trial exercise encourages critical thought in a myriad of ways. The students involved must critically analyze readings and lectures, yet also must construct a historical/legal case.

Again, all learning types are used, with a clear emphasis on creativity and historical analysis. Also common to both exercises is the impression that it will leave on the student, who often forgets what he or she has learned as soon as the course, and especially the exam, are over. The key goal inherent in a university education should be the creation of an 'educated person'. The fictional family and its variations aid the history instructor in this process, while providing skills that the student would not otherwise attain in the standard history curriculum as it is most commonly practiced. The students are given the tools they need and expect to succeed in the job market of today, and a greater understanding of history.

This is not to say that the student should be groomed as a middle management trainee, but rather as a lifelong learner. The student will still be trained as a historian, for the value of history as a discipline is clear: It is not, as Nietzsche would have it, a mere mummification of the past. The discipline should produce well-rounded individuals, able to research, to write, to think critically, and to present an argument verbally and visually. Even the undergraduate must be trained to turn a critical eye towards research and study, to shed new light on the past.

Thus we must not merely pour old wine into new bottles, but recognize innovative teaching methods, and grasp them in order to produce such well-rounded students. For the historian, the fictional family is the perfect vehicle with which to achieve the desired results.

References

Fukuyama, Francis. *The End of History and the Last Man.* New York: Avon Books, 1993.

Gold, Muriel. *The Fictional Family In Drama, Education andGroupwork.* Springfield: Charles C Thomas, 1991.

LaCapra, Dominick. *History and Criticism.* Ithaca: Cornell University Press, 1985.

LaCapra, Dominick and Steven L. Kaplan. (eds.) *Modern European Intellectual History.* Ithaca: Cornell University Press, 1982.

Nietzsche, Friedrich. *Untimely Meditations.* Cambridge: Cambridge University Press, 1997.

Endnotes

1. Friedrich Nietzsche. *Untimely Meditations.* Cambridge University Press. 1997, pp 74-75.

2. The Doyen of current Derridan historians is undoubtedly Dominick LaCapra. See for example: *History and Criticism* (Ithaca: Cornell University Press, 1985). The author perhaps most associated with "Postmodern history", however, is Haydn White {*Metahistory* (Baltimore, 1973), and *Tropics of Discourse* (Baltimore, 1978}.

3. Fukuyama, Francis. *The End of History and the Last Man.* New York: Avon Books, 1993.

4. One needs only to listen to any recent speech concerning education made by Canadian or American political leaders. The stress is continually placed upon the technological advancements of the computer industry, readying students with the skills needed for the new millennium, and engineering and the information technology industry as the most viable sources of employment. History, and the humanities in general, are seen as having no practical use, and therefore expendable.

5. See Dominick LaCapra and Steven L. Kaplan. (eds.) *Modern European Intellectual History: Reappraisals and New Perspectives.* Ithaca: Cornell University Press, 1982.

6. The authors take issue with the idea of contextual history: Both its practitioners - H. Stuart Hughes and Carl Schorske for example, and its advocates such as Quentin Skinner. The debate has spread from intellectual and cultural history, out into social history as well. None of these essays discuss curriculum or education, however.

7. I am no Gardner scholar, and as such am using the idea, and not the specifics here, as a starting point.

8. Muriel Gold. *The Fictional Family.* Springfield: Charles C Thomas, 1991, p. 1.

9. Ibid, p. 130

Chapter Seven:

Drama, Literature, and Multicultural Education

Muriel Gold

It has long been the preserve of the English teacher to help students learn to experience literature, or stories, more fully and deeply, particularly through understanding and identifying with various characters. This step can be difficult when characters in a story represent life experiences quite different from those of the students who encounter them. Yet the success or failure of students in "seeing through the eyes" of a character is a key factor affecting the quality of their experience with a story.

In recent years, new expectations have also cut across the curriculum, affecting all teachers regardless of their traditional subject matter expertise. One such new expectation is multicultural education, designed to help us all understand and at least tolerate, if not appreciate, the cultural and social differences among the North American population, differences which increasingly exist in close contact with each other in our cities and our classrooms. Another way to view the goals of multicultural education is as combating ignorance of others who are different from us, thus forcing us from fear of each other.

I propose that these two goals, of literature teaching and multicultural education, can be integrated and achieved together. In this chapter, I will describe how the FF technique (described in Chapter One) is used as a learning medium across the school curriculum. I will focus here specifically on its potential for offering students the experience of relating to a diversity of cultures at the same time as they explore the understanding of and identification with fictional characters.

Organization of Fictional Families

a) Roots

Before initiating the FF (when time permits) I initiate a preparatory exercise which sensitizes students, not only to their own backgrounds, but also to the backgrounds of their classmates. I ask each student to bring in one object and one food item which has special meaning for them and their 'real' families.

We sit in a circle on the floor, and each student in turn describes to the group h/er object, explains its significance, then passes it around for each person in the circle to touch and examine. Next, the student does the same with the food item. Each person receives a tiny sample of the food item to taste. This ritual encourages awareness of the cultural origins of others, and fosters mutual respect for each other's customs and values. Invariably, this exercise influences the formation of the fictional families. If time does not permit a ritual of this sort, before each group of students forms its families, I ask them to discuss with each other their backgrounds and cultures.

b) Formation of Fictional Families.

Normally in my work with FFs, the students have been **arbitrarily** divided into groups of five, then asked to form fictional families. For example, during a group movement exercise in which the whole class is involved, I might suddenly say FREEZE. Now turn to the four people next to you. Sit down on the floor with them. You will now comprise a fictional family.

c) Family Systems Exercise.

Robin Skynner in *FAMILIES and how to survive them*, (1983) describes to John Cleese, the British comic, an exercise used with family therapy trainees called the Family Systems Exercise. Its purpose is to demonstrate how people choose each other and fall in love.

He says this exercise should ideally be done before people in the group get to know each other. Each person is asked to choose someone in the room who either reminds h/er of someone in h/er own family or else gives h/er the impression that the person would have filled a gap in h/er own own family. No one is allowed to speak while in the process of selection. They walk around and look at one another and then move to the selected person. When they have chosen one another, they try to discover what influenced their choices. They are encouraged to compare their family backgrounds.

Next, each couple is asked to team up with another pair, in order to become a foursome. At this point they are asked to become a family for that one session. Together they select roles for themselves in the family. Then they discuss the qualities inherent to their family backgrounds which made them come to these decisions. Finally, they share their discoveries with the whole group. Inevitably, Skynner reports, they have all chosen people from families with very similar psychological profiles; he relates this phenomenon to the reasons why certain people are attracted to, and end up marrying one another.

"But what about the 'wall-flowers'?", John Cleese asks, the ones that nobody chose. And Skynner says that at first he was very worried that those not selected would all feel rejected. But when it came their turn to report family characteristics discovered in common, it turned out that they had all either been fostered or adopted children, or brought up in children's homes. They had all felt rejected in their early lives and somehow had picked each other out.

d) The Fictional Family and the Family Systems Exercise

I found this technique intriguing and decided to adapt it for my classes. Since my students already knew each other, instead of having them walk around looking at each other, I had them sit on the floor, close their eyes and visualize the people in the class. Then they were asked to move to the person(s) with whom they would be interacting. It worked extremely well, the students learned a lot about each other in a fun way. However, the following problem emerged which I later solved. Sometimes, for example, two or more people chose the same person and that person may have chosen someone other than the people who had chosen h/er. This was not a problem at the outset because they needed up to five people for their FFs. But one year about nine people grouped together and I had to quickly break them apart. (They were not happy about being torn apart.) This experience taught me that I must, before the choice began, tell them that groups could not be larger than five. That avoided future similar problems.

One year after the five "rejects" formed their group, and had their chance to talk with each other, they reported that the exercise "failed" because after "talking and talking" they found absolutely "nothing in common" in their backgrounds. "In that case, would you like me to divide you and put each of you with another group?", I asked. "Oh, no", they replied, "We all really got along. We would like to stay together." It seemed that they took pleasure in not "fitting in". It defined them as "individuals" distinct from the rest of the group. And so in the end, that was their common denominator.

e) Multicultural Grouping

Students make fictional family background choices centred around a particular ethnicity. There have been Italian, Greek, Jewish, Scottish, *etc.* in the various compositions. However, in a class centred on particular literary material, the teacher can direct the students to portray a particular variety of cultural backgrounds related to the characters in the story. For example, "The Ash Garden" by Canadian author Dennis Bock, centres around three protagonists, Emiko Amai, a Hiroshima survivor, Anton Boll, an expatriate German scientist who participated in the Manhattan Project, and Sophie, Anton's wife, a Jewish refugee. Each of the three students playing the central characters would form their own Fictional Family, and the other members of each family would be played by other students in the class. Some of these complementary characters might have been alluded to in the text, others are created from each fictional family's imagination. Enacting scenes from the characters' past, present and future lives helps students to experience, for example, a character's vulnerability in the face of racism. Enacting cross family scenes (one family interacts with another family) heightens the differences and similarities between cultures and offers insight, empathy, and understanding of others' backgrounds.

Parallel plot outlines can be offered as suggestions for improvisations before they even begin to study the actual text. When they finally read the text, they will have improvised a number of scenes related to the theme which will have helped them relate to the material.

g) Scheduling

The most common problem I encountered in FF classes was the conflicting schedules of students in a particular fictional family making it difficult for them to fulfil out-of-class assignments. Therefore at times I have asked them to state their availability before organizing the fictional families, then had them organize their groups around those who had similar schedules.

The above configurations describe a number of possibilities for organizing the fictional families-from random to structured. All

Muriel Gold, C.M., Ph.D.

arrangements can work. It is up to individual teachers to decide which way best suits them.

The Technique in Practice

I share here examples of the FF technique used in my university-based drama course to deal specifically with multicultural perspectives and issues.

Religious and cultural backgrounds chosen by the fictional families offer students opportunities to enact, view and subsequently discuss family processes in a socio-cultural context. For example: Paula, a black North American student created a fictional family character of 'mixed-race' named Zola. In the FF story line, before she was born, her mother and father had separated, and her mother spent a year in South Africa. During that year she had had an affair with a black African and had conceived a child, Zola. The affair did not last, and the mother subsequently brought that child back to Canada with her. (Interestingly enough, the student playing the mother is a Caucasian student of South African origin).

Paula presented a scene when her character (Zola) was five years old. In the scene she and her six-year-old Caucasian brother (Bryce) were first confronted with racism. An older boy began to taunt Bryce for playing with a 'nigger'. Bryce, who had never heard the term, beat up the boy and reassured his sister.

Paula subsequently explained in her journal that she wished to demonstrate to the predominantly White class, that it was only at this point that Zola 'became Black' indicating, she stressed, that people are not born with racism. Throughout the year, Zola and Bryce squabbled in a variety of scenes, but, as Paula pointed out, none of these arguments were racial in origin, but rather differences in opinion common to any brother or sister in any culture. In fact, class members mentioned that they enjoyed the bickering between Zola and Bryce because it reminded them of their own brothers and sisters. The

136

student playing Zola remarked that her 'familiarization strategy has been influential'.

It was obvious in class discussions that students enjoyed Zola as an individual. Her character is "neither stereo-typically negative nor stereo-typically comical," Paula wrote; she was simply a young woman who exhibited a free spirit and enjoyed life. She was not perfect. She was sometimes self-centred and spoiled. While she had the ability to adapt to settings all over the world, she never ignored the fact that she was Black.

In subsequent scenes, Zola travelled to Africa to search for her heritage. Members of the audience were able to identify with this search because they were aware of the fact that many adopted or illegitimate children wished to trace their natural parentage and culture.

After playing Zola over time in a number of different scenes, Paula wrote:

I have adopted the strategies of playwrights such as Lorraine Hansberry in creating a positive yet realistic Black character who is instrumental in the breaking of the 'wall', that being the trend of traditional Black stereotypes. When more playwrights (Black or White) deviate from this trend, the result will be a decrease in the need for Blacks to play stereotypical roles and an increase in demand for Blacks to play roles in integrated plays. If theatre is a reflection of society in its past, present and future forms, then one can say that the society of the future is represented by integrated theatre; a place where people of all races are able to understand each other and thus co-operate to produce something wonderful.

Zola

Unlike the black student who played Zola, many students choose to ignore their skin color when they play their FF roles, fitting into the family solely as individuals where differences in color or cultural backgrounds play no part.

Others adopt a particular heritage unlike the one that they, in real life, possess. For example, Paulanna, a Caucasian student, decided to take on the FF role of a teen-age Canadian native Indian who has been adopted by a Catholic Caucasian family. Many scenes revolved around the issues generated by this scenario. The adoptive parents had named her Mary, but she insisted on being called 'Starshine'. Her mother, a devout Catholic, wanted her to go to church Sundays. Heated arguments took place over this issue.

Eventually, like Zola, she decided to search for her 'real' (biological) mother. Her search took her to an Indian reserve in western Canada. The scene was presented by the family in Brechtian style. Cindi, playing Starshine's mother, described the scene in her journal:

> Our scene consisted of 'Starshine' running away to the reserve to find her real mom...We had a "changing of the mothers" to show the audience that we were in fact actors playing a part. I really enjoyed playing the two mothers because it gave me a chance to portray the differences between the two, both for the audience and for myself. I made a special effort to play each character as much to the extreme as their character would let them. Another Brechtian element we used was me accusing the audience of "stealing my babies and leaving liquor bottles in their cradles." The audience was the white world unaware of the native plight.

As mentioned in Chapter One, the FF begins within the context of Stanislavski (1961) and naturalism. We work first on inner technique. Students write autobiographies for their characters; they present and write inner monologues. Sense memory and visualization exercises are used as warm-ups prior to their performances. They also enact preceding scenes to the ones they are about to perform. Character preparation includes finding their FF characters' rhythm, and moving in role.

Stanislavski techniques are ultimately aimed to create rich, multi-faceted characters which will be believable on stage. Stanislavski actors strived to 'live' their roles through imagining themselves in sets of circumstances and relationships analogous to their textual characters.

Brecht and Social Issues

Having exposed the students to Stanislavski's naturalistic style where actors are required to identify with their characters' lives, I next introduce them to Brecht's alienation techniques where actors 'play' their characters rather than 'live' them (See Chapter One). Instead of disappearing into their roles, the actors retain their own individuality. When scenes threaten to become too sentimental the action is interrupted, sometimes by music or song, sometimes by a narrator who provides comment on the action taking place. This interruption or 'alienation' technique was implemented by Brecht as a strategy to limit emotional empathy. He wished the spectator to be engaged critically rather than emotionally so that his socio-political message would not be diluted by sentimentality. The FFs are now instructed to create scenes which reinforce social issues, often socio-cultural, relevant to their families. The actors select opposing points of view for their characters which result in dynamic scenarios and heated discussion about the many facets of racial and ethnic prejudices.

Fictional Families in Other Time Periods

Students may choose to create FFs in historical eras other than the present. Probably the most unusual choice was a group whose FF members decided that they were part of a 19th-century gypsy family who were circus performers. They called themselves The Nevsky family. The characters consisted of a fortune teller, apprentice magician, a juggler and a contortionist.

Their origins were Romanian, Yugoslavian and Russian. Although the FFs in my classes have represented a wide variety of family members, and sometimes placed their families in other decades such as the 1920s, 1960s or the year 2010, this was the first time that students had not only placed their family in another era, but also were tackling a family type about which they presumably knew little or nothing. Ernest, playing the father, was subsequently amazed to discover that he had gypsy origins. He wrote:

> That's it-the Nevsky family is no more. Yet it goes on and lives within each one of the family members. I discovered around Xmas time that my real family-my father, grandfather, and great-grandfather and grandmother-were actually circus performers juggling and tightrope walking in a turn-of-the-century circus in England. Odd, how art mirrors life.

The variety of scenes also offer students opportunities to introduce conflicts based on religious or cultural differences. For example, they are asked to play a scene in which their **FF character's secret** (which they have disclosed in their journals but not to anyone else) is revealed. The revealing of this secret is designed to evoke spontaneous responses from the FF members through the element of surprise. It additionally advances the plot. A student playing a widowed Jewish grandmother, named Molly Rosenberg, was able to introduce, through the secret, both social and religious issues. She wrote:

> A funny thing happened to Molly Rosenberg today. I hadn't pictured her in a relationship at this point in time, although I had planned to introduce the topic shortly in the form of a secret. However, one of the students asked (with tongue in cheek) whether Molly had a boyfriend. I suddenly felt indignant for all the seniors (who, younger people don't believe are sexually active) and I very quickly invented a man for her. Atta girl, Molly.

She continues:

> Promise never to tell? Here it is (my secret)! Molly Rosenberg put an ad in the companion's column of *The*

141

Gazette. Lois and the kids don't know. I'm not really sure that they'd understand. Anyway, what they don't know won't hurt them. I don't look seventy-two, and I was afraid that no one would answer a seventy-two-year-old's ad. It wasn't such a bad idea because I met someone who is what the kids call a HUNK. Sixty-five years old and doesn't look a day over sixty.

Agnes met him. She approves. I'm not sure why, but somehow I can't bring him home to Lois and the kids. But we go to his house. Do I have to say more? Arthur would die if he knew. Oh God. What did I just say?

P.S. He's not Jewish.

And the ad read:

[TRADITIONAL, attractive widow, 60, healthy, slim, athletic, has many interests. If you're clean cut, honest, intelligent, romantic, secure, a conversationalist, high standards, morals, values, would love to hear from you. 55-65, serious only. Recent photo. P.O. Box 2164]

Insight into their characters' behavioural patterns, and how they affect others, is gained through several techniques. Most often it is through playing the scene as their fictional family character and other times it is through observing members of their fictional families play scenes with other fictional family characters. Listening to the delivery of other fictional family characters' **inner monologues** offers them additional perspectives of how others view their characters. In the instance described below by Paulanna, playing "Starshine' it was a **family role-reversal** scene, in which another FF played her FF, that demonstrated to her her character's often negative behaviour. She wrote:

To see Amy play Starshine as the unreasonable whiny teenager who is constantly threatening to leave for the reserve if her petty demands aren't met (such as having maize on the picnic's menu) shed a whole new light on the picture.

The Fictional Family in Rehearsal of a Play

In addition to working with the FF in the acting class, I have used the technique in rehearsal situations both with collective creations and with written scripts. *The Ecstasy of Rita Joe* is a full-length play by Canadian playwright, George Ryga. The play revolves around the story of Rita Joe, a Canadian native, and the events which lead to her inevitable destruction. Placed in the framework of a trial by a white male magistrate, her story is gradually revealed in a series of intermittent flashbacks which end with her brutal murder by hooded killers.

Rita Joe and the Hooded Killers

The assortment of characters, white and native, were played by 17 actors who had auditioned and been cast for the roles using a non-traditional approach. For example, the white magistrate was played by a Canadian native; Rita Joe's native boyfriend, Jaimie Paul, was played by an Afro-Canadian; and the male social worker was played by a female.

The rehearsals took place over a six-week period. Of the 17 actors in the cast, eight played principal roles. In order to promote the actors' characterization process, intensify character interaction, and foster more profound character development, these eight actors were asked to write autobiographies, record character lines and to develop FFs in which they improvised past, present and future events in their characters' lives.

The nine supporting actors (each of whom played multiple parts in the play) attended FF rehearsals and participated in roles as required by the key actors for their improvisations, either as family characters alluded to in the text, imaginary family characters, or as characters outside the family.

The eight actors were asked to describe, in writing, the improvisations which they played at the FF rehearsals, and to record insights, if any, gained from playing each scene.

Following each improvisation, the actors were asked to remain on stage to discuss particular problems in the scene, establish clearer objectives to heighten the dramatic conflict, sustain a more direct focus, and help maintain moment-to-moment character interaction.

After replay, students articulated insights, if any, gained from the improvisation, and how these insights illuminated their characters' dialogue and actions in the play. They subsequently recorded their recollection of the experience in writing.

Many of the acting problems revolved around their difficulties with understanding the emotional context of the characters' biased attitudes toward each other's cultures. For example, a series of FF past scenes helped the actors playing native characters to understand their behaviour toward whites in the text. Similarly, the actors playing Caucasian characters were helped to understand their behaviour toward the natives.

While the last example illustrates the FF technique applied to the performance of a play, it can be readily adapted to the reading of prose literature as a means of helping students gain deeper insight into various characters in a text. Indeed, the technique also serves as a strong base for a wide range of writing, from journal entries to stories based on the FF characters and on improvised scenes. Furthermore, while I have focused here on narrative within the English curriculum the technique can be utilized for similar multicultural issues in most other disciplines such as social studies, moral and religious education and history.

Application of the Methodology to Literary Texts

The FF approach can be used with literary texts in the school curriculum. For example, each student selects a character from the novel or short story which the class is studying and creates a fictional family for their character.

First they record in writing (or underline) all the character lines *i.e.,* lines that reveal some aspect of the character's personality or psyche. These lines include comments by the given character, by other characters in the text, by the author (or narrator) and by the given character about others in the play.

They write their selected characters' autobiographies. In these autobiographies they combine the historical data given about their characters in the text with their own imaginative details (those not given in the text). They continue to add to their autobiographies as they discover additional dimensions to their characters and to their characters' fictional families throughout the study of the book. They can make scrapbooks or include in their journals photos of their characters' past lives from infancy to the time they died. They design their characters' family homes.

Actors can independently prepare chronological action charts of their characters' life events to demonstrate the chronological relationship to the other characters. This chart enables the actors to develop the social, psychological, personal and emotional relationships which lead to credible character interaction. Students can improvise scenes that either take place in the story and/or invent scenes alluded to in the text. These invented scenes may have taken place in the character's past, present or future life. Dramatic enactments of events in their characters' lives will add insight not only into their own character's psyche, but also into the psyche of the characters selected by others.

Toward a Cross-Cultural Perspective Through Drama

In conclusion, the FF was designed as an actor-training technique. However, it can accomplish therapeutic goals in the areas of human development. From a cultural perspective, it can be an effective medium through which to sensitize students to cultural differences, to help them develop an openness to cultural variability and to strengthen a sense of positive cultural self-identity.

McGoldrick (1987) tells us that 'all human beings experience life on the basis of their own cultural values and assumptions, most of which are outside their awareness. Unless confronted by others whose values differ from our own, we inevitably see the world through our own 'cultural filters', often persisting in established views despite clear information to the contrary'. And she points out, 'Ethnicity is deeply tied to the family through which it is transmitted'. She goes on to say that 'it seems natural that an interest in families should lead to an interest in ethnicity, and *vice versa*, yet this area has been ignored in clinical teaching and research'.

The FF technique in improvisational drama is one means by which these topics and issues can be explored.

Other Topics

This chapter has dealt with examples dealing specifically with diversity and multiculturalism. However, a wide variety of social issues appear in the scenarios of the fictional families such as ageism, sexual assault, mental and physical disabilities, death, divorce, substance abuse, bullying, step-families and teen-age suicide. These topics should be inseparable from the work with FF. The teacher should seize this precious opportunity to generate exploration of topics vital to students' personal growth and transformation into mature, responsible, autonomous beings.

References

Gold, Muriel (1988). The Fictional Family in actor training. *Speech and Drama,* **37**(2),9-18. Oxford: Society of Teachers of Speech and Drama

Gold, Muriel (1991). *The Fictional Family in Drama, Education and Groupwork.* Springfield, Ill. Charles C. Thomas

Gold, Muriel (March 1993) The Fictional Family: A Multi-Cultural Perspective. *English Quarterly* 25 (1), 26-29. Calgary, Alberta. Canadian Council of Teachers of English and Language Arts

Gold, Muriel (2000) *Therapy Through Drama. The Fictional Family.* Springfield, Ill. Charles C. Thomas

Landy, Robert. (1986). *Drama Therapy: Concepts and Practices.* Springfield, Ill.Charles C. Thomas

McGoldrick, Monica. (1982). Normal Families: An Ethnic Perspective. In Froma Walsh,(Ed.). *Normal Family Processes.* New York: The Guilford Press.

Skynner, Robin and John Cleese (1984). *FAMILIES and how to survive them.* New York. Oxford University Press.

Stanislavski, Constantin. (1961). *Creating a Role.* New York: Theatre Arts.

Willett, John. (Ed.) (1964). *Brecht on Theatre.* New York: Hill and Wang.

Chapter Eight:

Exploring Gender Issues in the Drama Class

Muriel Gold

Despite the widespread acknowledgement of the importance of dealing with gender issues in education, their treatment in schooling still remains a problematic arena. In schooling generally, with the exception of a few women's studies courses at the post-secondary level, there are virtually no separate courses on gender issues specifically. Rather, most educational institutions have adopted broad, gender equity policies that should have an effect on all aspects of schooling-policies, curriculum, learning materials, teaching approaches, school organization, hiring and salary practices, and so on. Yet implementation of such policies, especially as they affect life in classrooms, is often left up to individual teachers, with predictably spotty results. In addition, few educational institutions conduct regular assessments of the implementation of such policies, unless pressured to do so by feminist groups.

Material on feminist theatre (Case, 1988; Dolan, 1988; Bassnett-McGuire, 1984; Todd, 1984) is becoming more readily accessible. However, it is difficult to find material connecting gender and acting pedagogy. One might conclude, therefore, that gender in the acting class is not sufficiently addressed. A notable exception may be Rhonda Blair

(1992) whose theatre training technique is designed within a feminist pedagogy. Deanna Banz Jent, in her doctoral dissertation, *Sex Roles in the Acting Class: Exploring the Effects of Actor Training on Nonverbal Gender Display*, attempts to pave the way for altering theatre educators and acting teachers' perspectives on acting pedagogy. However, hers is a foundational study based on observations of a narrow sample and is not focused on models for new acting techniques.

Similarly, books focused on gender issues in family dynamics are not very common (Dell, 1989; Laird, 1988; Wilcoxon, 1989). In her article about women and ritual in family therapy, Laird stresses the fact that the powerful relationship between gender and ritual in family therapy has not yet been addressed. She points out that sex, a biological fact, must be distinguished from gender, a socio-cultural construction. Wilcoxon agrees that gender issues for marital and family practitioners are not being dealt with, resulting in a lack of appreciation for gender differences (Wilcoxon, 1989).

Fictional Family Roles

The roles selected and the situations presented by the fictional families offer students opportunities to enact, view and subsequently discuss characteristic male and female roles, identify sexual stereotypical attitudes and behaviour, take note of gender discrimination and develop the potential, through their characters, to take action which can lead to empowerment. Since the acting pedagogy takes place within the framework of the family, the relationship between these roles and marital and family interaction can be explored.

Male-female Hierarchy

For example: A student playing the role of Bridget was constantly being condescended to, and discriminated by, the four male members of her fictional family. Neither the student nor the character was aware of the discrimination until the topic was raised in post-performance discussion.

Muriel Gold, C.M., Ph.D.

Both actor and audience had accepted the male-female hierarchy as that which takes place in 'real life'. Subsequent to the audience response, Bridget began to assert herself in future scenes. This change not only ameliorated her work as an actress and created more dynamic scenes, but also as one student remarked, "The element of surprise at ourselves at having accepted the male-female dominant situation made a greater impact than if we had been prepared in advance to learn about feminism, because it personalized the issue."

Sexual Assault

A second example occurred when Connie, a teen-age girl, attempted to reveal to her father, Stan, that her 'friend' had been date raped. Stan's response, "What was she wearing?" evoked shocks from the audience particularly because Stan, a high school teacher, was a character whom everyone had grown to love. A powerful discussion ensued which sensitized audience members to the gross misconceptions of sexual assault.

In an equally provocative scene, Dean, an 18-year-old university freshman, confessed to his sister that he thought he "may have" raped a female student at a fraternity party while under the influence of alcohol. He was upset, remorseful, ashamed and extremely anxious that his younger brother who admired him not find out about this event. Although many students have enacted scenes surrounding the issue of sexual assault, this was the first time in my experience that a male tackled the issue from the perpetrator's perspective. In post-performance discussion, the actor playing Dean stated that his character had not in fact raped the girl but he had "taken advantage of her, and that was equally bad".

The most powerful example of sensitizing students to the effects of date rape was exhibited by a female student who enacted the role of Tinitja, daugher of a Jewish mother and black South African father. During the series of FF scenarios, Tinitja transforms from a happy, model daughter to a problematic young woman exhibiting unhealthy behavioural symptoms such as anorexia, heavy smoking, deliberate wilfulness toward her family, and general malaise. When eventually she gets up the courage to confide in her mother, and gains her mother's support, a strong message is delivered to the audience about the need of rape survivors to disclose their stories and receive validation.

In the final FF scene (presented in Kabuki style) Tinitja, the warrior, is able to confront and deliver retribution to her abuser. Notably, her fictional family members, unbeknownst to her character (but not to the actor) have followed her into the forest, to ensure that she was safe, but they left it to her to go alone on her mission. It was clear to the participants and the spectators that in this action of empowerment Tinitja was on the road to healing. As Tinitja, the warrior, overcame and slew her perpetrator, the class became trusted witnesses to her disclosure and revenge, and were moved toward real-life empathy to the survivor.

Her FF matriarch, Johanna, had trained and counselled her in this act because she wished "to transmit the art of warriorship to my daughter so she can gain enough confidence and skill to join the lineage of our ancestors who have fought the 'eternal' battle against injustice."

And from Tinitja's journal:

> Do you understand what it means to be violated? I am talking about physical violation?...what it means to lose complete control over one's body. You were so wrongfully inside of me. You broke into my self -- my soul -- and took away all its meaning and life. (03/11/92)

Tinitja, Kabuki warrior slaying perpetrator

The student who played the mother offered the following comments about the audience's perspective:

> Buried myths of strong matriarchal boundary setters and protectors are re-emerging in life and in the theatre. No longer content to watch the passive "carrying-off" of women by Zeus-like characters, audiences of today need to see, and collectively celebrate in rituals, powerful females who set boundaries, refuse to be victims, and stand up to violent men. In standing up, these women restore the sacred hoop of life, affirming proper relationships for all of us.

On the other side of the coin, in performances which touch on autobiographical material, the act of having one's absolutely appropriate rage witnessed and sanctioned publicly in the drama space, may allow one to break out of the silence, depression and individual "self-blame" pattern which often results from sexual assault.

In such performances, the audience can be seen to take on the role of a compassionate restorative community sharing in the protagonist's heroic journey, sharing in a sense of outrage for what never should have happened to them (whether they are male or female). Most audience members know how hard it is for a person who has been sexually assaulted to get to a place of rage. That place of rage as it relates to setting boundaries is potentially a profound and healing place.

In the fictional world of "as if", Tinitja was able to mete out her sense of restorative justice in a supportive arena. In the final scene, the audience was with her all the way, holding their breath as she confronted and slew her aggressor, celebrating her symbolic victory as she transitioned from victim-hood back into her sacred womanhood which was powerful confident, sexual and free.

During the transition she was able to release an enormous amount of rage in a safe and contained way without negative consequence. As she lifted her sword of defiance in a final, powerful gesture, rather than becoming a symbolic brute, she fulfilled an ancient archetype, becoming for us *a sacred keeper of boundaries, a protector* to contend with and *a guardian of the feminine sexual body.* As an audience member, it can be a privilege to watch such an unfolding, for seeing one person strengthen the boundary, strengthens us all.

Fictional Family and Feminist Theatre

Other issues such as lesbianism, family violence, eating disorders and other more subtle manifestations of sex differentiation appear in the case studies of many of the fictional family characters. A student argued in her paper that: "the fictional family technique has a stronger impact than feminist theatre because of its use of interesting poly-dimensional characters as opposed to the flat stereotype characters often found in feminist theatre".

Displays of Emotion - Female vs Male

FF scenes which contain controversial emotional issues provoke discussion of contrasting cultural and gender approaches to human behaviour. For example, a student playing the role of Riki, enacted a scene which had taken place ten years in the past. Standing at his mother's grave following her funeral, he held back his tears because he said he had to be 'strong like a man'. A discussion ensued about which took more courage, containing or displaying emotion.

In another scenario, a student playing the role of Jackie at ten years of age, was furious with her mother who insisted she wear a dress and sit quietly, while her twin brother was allowed to play in the puddles. The inequity was noted by the class in post-performance evaluation.

Riki at his mother's grave

Feminism and Black Female Actors

Religious and cultural backgrounds chosen by the FFs offer students opportunities to interact in a socio-cultural context where they can deal with issues of racism and class bias. According to Case (1988), there has been little material published about feminism and black women in theatre. It appears that many black female actors are involved in black issues, but few explore these issues in the context of feminism.

Chapter Seven describes how Paula, a black North American student created a FF character of 'mixed-race' named Zola through which she explored the issues of racism. Zola experienced a variety of situations and settings. However, no matter where she travelled or whom she encountered, she strongly maintained her identity as a black woman.

Also described in Chapter Seven is a student who portrayed a native Indian girl adopted by a Catholic Caucasian family. Her search for her 'real' (biological) mother on an Indian reserve in western Canada led to a scene which sensitized both actors and audience to the opposing perspectives of mother figures from different cultures. The native mother accused the white audience of "stealing my babies and leaving liquor bottles in their cradles." Issues of adoption and rights of the birth mother offered an additional dimension to discussion of the scene.

> The impact of religion and cultural mythology on women's self-concept and the impact of sexual repression in a patriarchal society can assist people to become culturally aware and lead them to effect social change (Strongylu, 1990).

The FF combines actor-training methodology (from Stanislavski to Brecht to Beckett) with family dynamics. The variety of relationships portrayed in the fictional families-sex roles and marital interaction, sex roles and parent-child interaction-can provide conducive settings for a diversity of evocative material. In a group of students from diverse family backgrounds, students will have their own personal perceptions of family relationships. This variety of perspectives is evident in performance, in post-performance discussions and in journal writing.

Ageism

Students who play much older characters have an opportunity to explore the personal concerns of this population. In so doing, they can help to dispel negative myths of aging. They can transform older women who may be traditionally played as lonely and unfulfilled into independent individuals with their own friends and own lives. Most women's lives are not linear. Women often interrupt or commence careers late to concentrate on family. Therefore issues of making new starts, building self-confidence, finding courage at various stages of their lives are prominent problems for women. The FF scenes provide students with the opportunity of depicting this circular apect of womens' lives, and effecting change. According to Walsh (1980), the majority of adults over 65 live with family and not in institutions as is commonly believed. McGoldrick and Carter (1982) state that the older adult needs to be encouraged to become independent by family members especially when the spouse is gone. Women, who have spent their lives as nurturers, are particularly vulnerable and are often unable to relinquish their status with their children. Since older adults are generally not valued in our society, it is often difficult for their children and grandchildren to view them as models. According to McGoldrick and Carter, family members need to negotiate a new balance in their relationships that will be more appropriate for the present.

Hopes and Dreams

Before presenting their future scenes, students are asked to write their characters' hopes and dreams for the future. The character of 72-year-old Molly Rosenberg involved not only religious and cultural issues (see Chapter Seven) but also issues of ageism and feminism.

> You know, I get scared when I have to think about the future. The years are flying by so fast, I wonder how much of a future I have left. Naturally, the first thing that I think about is my health. How long can I stay healthy? Already I have a hip that doesn't do what it's supposed to. I eat properly. I exercise. But, old age is old age. I see what happens at the Centre. I saw what happened to my Arthur. One minute they're fine, the next minute, they're dead. Without warning-just like that. Let me tell you

–that's probably the best way. When I die, please God, let it be in my sleep. Imagine if I was sick for a long time and Lois [my daughter-in-law] would have to take care of me or-God forbid-she would put me in a home.

Do you think it's too late for me to sell my writing? Lois keeps telling me No-but nothing has happened yet. I wish more older women would be interested in Feminism...Agnes and I were thinking of starting a newsletter designed especially for older women who don't believe that every female should be able to bake apple pies and who understand when their grandchildren would rather work than have babies.

Although I've been faithful with my meditations-I would love to have the courage to go to an Ashram in India. Maybe I'll get over my fear. What happens if I get there and I get sick? Do you think that I'm too old to try? Who knows-maybe, next year Agnes and I can go with a group. I hate groups. Maybe I won't go and that's that.

However, Molly Rosenberg subsequently played a scene with her grandaughter at the airport. She gave the impression that it was Lisa, her grandaughter who was going on a trip. But in a surprise ending the audience discovered that Molly was in fact the one who was fulfilling her dream of visiting India.

Scenes in the Future
Scenes which take place in the future allow students to alter their status in their FFs. This shift in status provides them with the opportunity to envisage new possibilities for overcoming obstacles and to initiate change. For example, a student playing Isabella, the dependent wife of a radio station owner, who had sacrificed her career as a singer to

become homemaker, convinced her husband following his heart attack, to sell the station. In subsequent scenes she became more assertive and independent gradually gaining the respect from her family which she had previously been unable to attain.

Lesbianism

A FF character called Raisa had divorced her husband and moved in with her sister Hannah's family. Since Hannah was Mayor of Tokyo, Ontario, the small town in which they lived, Raisa and her teen-age daughter were relegated to low status family members. For weeks the audience was very sympathetic toward the character until in a scene ten years in the future, Raisa revealed her intimate relationship with another woman. The instinctive reaction by the audience was, as one student remarked in her journal, "juvenile and perhaps even old fashioned. The reality of homosexuality was on the whole taken lightly and more as a joke than an insight into Raisa's personality."

She went on to say that after weeks of believing that Raisa's husband was partly responsible for the divorce, the sympathy was reversed and Raisa became villain. This type of response is corroborated by art therapist Ellis (1989) who states that "lesbian experience continues to be viewed with fear or hatred or is instead denied." On reflection through post-performance discussion, journal writing and the viewing of subsequent scenes which allowed Raisa's family to validate her sense of identity, students' sensitivity to the issue of lesbianism was heightened.

The Long-Term Unattached-Autonomy and Intimacy

A student playing Claudia had her character "stuck" in a loveless and unfulfilling marriage because Claudia was afraid of living alone. Now 42 years old and pregnant for the first time in her life, she packs her bags and finds the courage to commence a new life. As an autonomous woman, she is able to interact positively with her former husband and maintain an egalitarian relationship with her stepdaughters.

In her doctoral study of the long-term unattached, Siegel (1989) suggests that new models for intimate relationships are needed which demonstrate that autonomy and intimacy are not mutually exclusive. The enactment and viewing of a variety of solutions to marital and family relationship problems heighten students' awareness of problem solving in this context.

Divorce

Students are free to choose a variety of topics when they write papers based on their FF experience. One such paper examined *Divorce in the Fictional Family*. The student noted that three of the four fictional families had ended in divorce and were headed by a single custodial parent-two of whom were men. She interviewed six members of the fictional families (the three adults and three of their children) in an attempt to gain an understanding of how divorce affected them, and to evaluate whether or not the students were accurately portraying divorce.

Interestingly, she discovered that in all cases, it was the woman who had initiated the divorce, each for a different reason. The first because she did not want to move from Toronto when her husband was offered a job in Portland; and also because, by his own admission, he was "a difficult man to live with". The second left, her husband suspected, because she was no longer in love with him and was having an extra-marital affair. The third stated that she was forced to divorce her husband because he was sexually abusing their three-year-old daughter and thus she had a moral and legal responsibility to leave her abusive husband. She felt a sense of relief to leave the city and escape to a life where she could care for her children in peace.

The student examined the differences in the ways that men and women react to separation. Supporting her interviews with research materials on the topic of divorce (e.g. Price, Sharon and McKenry, 1988) she found that men were more vulnerable to separation because they suppressed their feelings, and used buffers such as work or social activity in an attempt to avoid the problem. Women tended to be prouder and angrier, but confronted their problems head on. They focused their energy on providing their children with a nurturing and loving home environment. Their principal stress often arose from insufficient economic resources.

The student concluded that many of the characters' portrayals of divorce were "extremely realistic."

Females in Business Management

Maria, a FF character in a traditional Italian family, tried in vain to convince her father, Mario, who was running a successful contracting business, that she was capable of joining him. Mario, on the other hand, kept insisting that his son, John, join him in the business and eventually take it over. The son, however, had no interest in business and wanted to continue his liberal arts education. The father's viewpoint caused considerable anger and anxiety in the family, and a number of scenes harped on this serious controversy.

Fictional Family Houses

Students make models of their fictional families' houses and present them as a group to the other families. In one presentation Zak, Isabella's husband, dominated the presentation by showing off "his" house and presenting his "wife's" room. Isabella immediately took exception to being referred to as "wife", and the audience became involved in a discussion pertaining to leadership, independence and possessiveness.

Fictional Families and Possibilities for Change

In a textual role, actors have to work within the limits of a character created by a playwright. They can interpret, add imaginative details, discover and create additional dimensions to the role, but ultimately they are confined to the words, the dialogue, the story and the general framework of the author's work.

Stanislavski, in his teachings and directing, dealt with character creation in the context of textual roles. His books deal with the actor's approach to a variety of famous authors' texts-such as Chekhov, Shakespeare, Ibsen and Molière.

> How can she [a female actor] assert herself on and off-stage when her gender role keeps her quiet and stationary? Being able to perform gender roles is fine for an actress as long as she only wants to be cast as Ophelia or Blanche, but what if she wants to play a non-traditional role...female actors need to find ways to break out of limiting gender stereotypes. (Jent, 1989, page 188).

In the FF technique, the character is created, not from a written text, but from the actor's imagination. It is born from the imagination and placed in a family unit. This family unit is created from the joint imagination of a small group of actors.

Therefore possibilities for change are not confined to the author's text but scenarios can be altered according to the personal growth of the actor and character. Because the FF is not designed primarily as a gender-based technique (although it can use gender as its focus) its lack of label may be its strength. Attaching a feminist label to an artistic work can tend to dominate the aesthetic and alienate otherwise interested spectators and participants.

Gender and Scripted Plays using Fictional Family

There are many plays which afford opportunity for students to become attuned to feminist issues. In teaching a course in Modern Drama, I have frequently used Ibsen's "A Doll's House" as a classic example of 19th century attitudes toward women and morality. At first read, students are filled with derision at Nora's behaviour as her husband Helmer's "doll-child" in the first scenes of the play. Over the course of the story, they discover that women like Nora had no power, that they were in fact treated as children not only by their husbands but also by society. At the end of the play when Nora leaves Helmer, it seems to them it is something she should have done from the outset. Later they come to realize the obstacles in her path, and the enormous courage it took for her to depart from all that was familiar to her. They also learn that Ibsen's ending was a departure from the dramatic literature of the day which generally ended in dramatic closures which raised no questions of conduct or morality.

Research Topics

As with all plays they study I give students a list of topics to research (see end of chapter) which will help them place Nora's story in the context of the times. Next they select their roles, create fictional families for their characters composed of: *a)* the characters in the play, *b)* those alluded to in the text but who do not appear in the play, and *c)* imaginary characters. They design FF trees and their character diaries are ongoing as they enact the various scenarios. Some students place these scenes in the era of the play, others take the same situation and create improvisations in contemporary society to discover what changes occur in characters' behaviours.

As Tracy Davis points out:

> When Nora (the heroine of Ibsen's *A Doll's House)* left her home and family "to think things out for herself" and "get things clear", the noise of the door slamming behind her is said to have reverberated throughout Europe. Since 1879, hundreds of thousands of women have been moved by Nora's plight and inspired by her resolve to understand what made her as she was, to seek a self-defined truth, and to win independence from her male master. (Davis, p. 218, 1988)

Muriel Gold, C.M., Ph.D.

A frequent topic of discussion revolves around what happens to Nora after she leaves her home and children. Students are encouraged to enact these scenes either as improvisations or from their own written scripts. These enactments provide a myriad of possibilities for the characters. Does Nora find her way and become empowered? Or does she live the rest of her days abandoned and in poverty? Does Helmer see the error of his ways, and change, allowing her to return home and live "happily ever after"? Or does Nora, realizing she can't make it on her own, cave in and return to a home in which the male-female hierarchy remains unchanged? Re-workings of the final scene consider why or if Nora will leave, or stay in, her doll's house.

In any case, the play gives teacher and students evocative material to discuss "priorities and perceptions of the evolving feminist movement traced back to Ibsen's characters and situations" (Ibid, 1988). The enacting of FF past scenarios-Nora at home with her father, Nora at school with her friend, Christine Lynde, Nora meets Helmer, *etc.*, *etc.*-are all possibilities for further exploration of gender issues.

As Davis concludes:

> No one has yet resolved the sexual and gender differences, discovered the "miracle of miracles" , made a motion for adoption of a final agenda, or moved for closure of the debate. Clearly, the questions and discussion that *A Doll's House* can reflect are still evolving. (p. 226)

FF Character Questions
An example of a secondary student's responses to the FF character questions described in Chapter Four follows:

Nora Helmer
My childhood was like living in a playground.

My father was the only parent I had except if you count my nurse. My father was a very upright man.

I had no friends because I was isolated in my home.

My father was vice-president of a company which produced hand paper.

My grandparents were decent employees of the same company that my father worked for.

I often felt lonely because my father would not let me go out very much.

I am a very social person. I like being around people.

I always dreamed of having my own doll's house.

I am very healthy.

I like my father, husband, and children. But I am starting to dislike my husband because I realize many things about my life.

I like the way I look-beautiful.

Reality makes me sad.

I am happy when I play with my children.

I am thin, have green eyes, brown hair and white skin.

I think people think of me as a child.

I see myself as someone who plays being a child, but I am a tricky person.

To deal with conflict, I try to make others see who I truly am.

My heart is the most sensitive part of my body.

My chest, where my heart is, is the part that leads my body when I move.

My physical mannerism is my arms.

The death of my mother was the most significant incident in my life. If she had been here, my life would have been different.

My father's brother had a great influence on my life, he
and his doles.

Suggested Research Topics

1. Ibsen's Biography

2. The literature of the period in which the play takes place

3. Social history of the period in which the play takes place

4. Social mores and manners of the period in which the play takes
place

5. Critical reviews of the play

6. Relevance of the play to the '90s

7. The portrayal of women in the play

8. Design the costumes for the play

9. The visual arts of the period in which the play takes place

10. Politics of the period in which the play takes place

11. The portrayal of men in the play

12. Architecture of the period in which the play takes place

How would university instructors and/ or teachers set about introducing FF in relation to gender issues?

Ritual

In Chapter Seven I described a ritual which I sometimes use before
asking students to form fictional families. I ask each student to bring in
an object and a sample food representing their family's ethnic traditions.
The emphasis is on learning about each other's cultures.

Similarly, the teacher who wishes to focus on gender issues could
implement the same exercise, with the request that the object and food
sample represent female family members and/or their relationship
with their families. This stipulation initiates students to talk about the

characteristics of the females in their families, and issues of gender would naturally emerge. Families could be families of origin or present families.

The teacher should be part of the group, also bringing in an object and food. However, the teacher can also act as facilitator asking pertinent questions to help students reflect on the implications of their descriptions, and to help them notice whether general characteristic relationships emerge between males and females in the family and in society.

The Fictional Family Scenarios

The emphasis on gender awareness need not be limited to the introduction of FF. As seen from the numerous examples given in this chapter, the opportunity for discussion of gender arises frequently in the scenarios. However, if the teacher wishes the class to focus specifically on gender issues, then the teacher can suggest that topics of gender be incorporated in their improvisations and in their written scenes. For example, a fictional family performing a scene in Brechtian style, selected as their title "Rebellion against the Mother or Letting Go of the Mother."

The son, who had a love-hate relationship with his mother, used a baseball bat to bash "the hell out of" a glass-filled bag symbolizing "mom". The student playing the son described, in his journal, the scene as 'pretty intense' and that *his character* "was finally released and felt free". And that he, as actor, found the experience to be "a great cathartic release", and wondered why he 'found it much easier to express the emotion of anger and hatred rather than love and beauty." He described the context of the scene which followed:

> Antonia [the mother] was leaving the household in order
> to seek wealth in the city. That's why the music she
> chose was "money" by "Pink Floyd." She got dressed up
> in fancy clothes, put her money-belt on and left for the

city. Sharon [daughter] became the innocent victim who was trying to reach out to the other family members in hopes of re-uniting us, but no one would listen to her. Andrew [the elder son] became the narrator who recited the two poems by Amelia and Nimike [the younger children].

And of course there was mom who got pieces of her clothes ripped apart (symbolizing the ripping away of pieces of herself). Also a paradox in which, while we tear her apart, we are taking a piece of her with us to keep for ourselves and to always remember her by - it was not completely a violent act.

Fictional Family Sculpture

A second example of a scenario was inspired by the FF sculpture (see Chapter One) created to demonstrate a social issue. In the sculpture Nathan, the Father, is standing on top of a table, marking the top of the hierarchy, while Mary, the Mother, lies on the floor. Janice, the daughter is sitting on the floor, and Scott, the son, is sitting on the table. The sculpture is followed by a scene is which Janice dethrones her father, declaring that she is "Queen of the Castle". A student describes the scene.

Our socio-political issue for our Brechtian family scene was gender issues which arose from our family sculpture. More specifically that women's place is in the home. Our message was that women have an equal role in society, which we would show through satire...

We felt that a university audience would be the most appropriate, yet we needed a group that was sexist to make it into a learning experience. That was how we came up with the Engineering Society, a group which we feel has yet to achieve sexual equality.

We thought of several alienation effects, Mary would have a white face to show fear, Nathan would be covered in black to show evil, and have a picture of a pig on his chest, Janice would put red on just before her final scene to show anger as well and wear a tank top with a pink triangle to show she was gay.

We also thought of the huge banner which stated, It's 7 p.m., have you kicked your mother today?

Pete would be the ideal narrator since he was good at delivering monologues.

Before preparing their Brechtian FF scenes, I ask students to choose an (imaginary) **audience** for which they will be staging their scene. Brecht believed that society's outlook could be changed and that the theatre was a powerful vehicle to execute that change. I ask students to select an audience which would benefit from the scene's message. In the above example, the choice was the Engineering Society, viewed by the students as requiring education in the area of gender awareness. In other scenarios, students have chosen audiences of unwed mothers for topics of adoption, fraternity societies for issues of rape, alcoholics anonymous for issues of domestic violence.

Drama versus Discourse

As pointed out at the beginning of this chapter, material connecting gender and acting pedagogy is difficult to find. Also there are not many courses that focus solely on gender issues. Those that do are found in Women's Studies programs geared to be conversational rather than dramatic. Yet dramatic techniques have proven to be an effective and powerful means to create awareness in a variety of disciplines. This chapter has provided examples of how the FF improvisations and FF scripts have engendered (no pun intended) discoveries of gender biases. However, in retrospect it may be helpful to the teacher if I offer how some specific FF techniques can be used in this context.

Fictional Family Dramatic Techniques

Conflicts and Objectives

I suggest to students, from the beginning, that their improvisations and scenes be structured around a FF conflict issue designed to quickly provoke emotional interaction between fictional family members, and that each member create a dynamic objective. In working with gender, the conflict will be centered around this topic. The issue need not be complex. Some examples might be:

a) a daughter wishes to borrow the family car to attend a concert with friends. Her brother says he needs it because he has a date, and a male *has* to show up for his date with a car. (This could be the FF conflict in pairs; followed by the two parents taking sides)

b) two students, one male, one female, return home from school. The daughter is expected to help prepare dinner and clean up afterwards, while the son takes out the garbage and is then free to study or meet friends. An angry daughter rebels resulting in what could be the *FF crisis scene. Inner monologues* might follow after which a *re-enactment* could take place whereby more equitable arrangements are agreed upon.

c) it is morning (this could be the *FF breakfast scene*) in which two working parents are getting ready to leave for work. The mother wakes the children, prepares their breakfast, prepares their lunch meal for them to take to school, makes sure they have all their belongings and are out of the house on time, makes the beds, showers, dresses, has breakfast, is about to leave for work. Her husband awakes, goes for a run before breakfast, showers, has breakfast, is about to leave for work when his wife confronts him about sharing of responsibilities.

Dramatic Interventions

There are several means of intervention. The challenge for the teacher is to sense the appropriate moment and manner of intervention. One does not want to impede the dramatic flow. The objective is to *enhance* the dramatic flow if the scene is stagnating or losing focus.

Interrupting the Action

When I wish to interrupt the action I call out FREEZE. That way the actors stay focused and in character. My suggestions and questions are normally to the *characters* rather than the actors.

a) I remind them of their objectives "What do you (your character) *want* at this moment? Face (*e.g.*) your mother or sister and tell her what it is you want from her. Keep repeating it until she listens and HEARS what it is you are saying.

b) Or, after instructing the actors to freeze, I might ask the *audience* to give input. For example, when the FF character Bridget came home from a full day's work, she immediately ran into the kitchen to prepare meals for the men in her fictional family who were lolling around the TV relaxing before dinner. When I stopped the action to ask the class what they thought of this arrangement, consciousness was raised about housework responsibilities and sharing of household duties between genders. This awareness filtered in, not only to the future scenes in Bridget's fictional family, where she became more assertive and the males more sensitive, but also to scenes in the other fictional families.

c) Another technique I use is what Viola Spolin (1960) calls *'side coaching'*. This technique is especially useful when one wants to help actors to stay focused on their objectives. It works well too when the teacher wants the actors to either accelerate or slow down a scene in progress.

Inner Monologues

As described in earlier chapters, inner monologues are useful tools which can be applied before, during, or following a scene. In a gender-awareness setting, the monologues will be focused on characters' perceptions of themes such gender inequalities, gender insensitivity and victimization.

Role Reversal

By reversing roles, actors can play out, not only their own FF role, but can also play characters with whom they are interacting. Putting one's self in another's shoes can quickly lend practical and emotional insight to another's situation resulting in the discovery of one's inappropriate behaviour and sometimes unconscious prejudice toward another. I have even used "whole FF reversals" in which one fictional family can view their own attitudes and behaviours as portrayed by another fictional family. This technique is not only hilarious but also enlightening.

The Double

In "Doubling" (a term borrowed from psychodrama) one actor speaks for another character. For example, if a character is unable to express her sense of victimization or frustration, the actor playing her inner thoughts can express her feelings for her. The character can then be asked to repeat what her double is saying, (if this is the true representation of her thoughts) thereby helping her to express her emotions, become more assertive and gain self-confidence. It is an accepted active technique to effectively counter resistance in families and individuals.

Status Re-enactment

Another dramatic technique I use involves use of status. When a male dominates a situation creating anxiety or fear on the part of the female, I will ask the female to stand on a chair while the male is asked to crouch beside her. They then re-enact the scene. Or, in a more extreme situation, I might ask the male to lie down on the floor with the female placing her foot on the prostate body. The prostate male must struggle to get up while the female must keep her foot firmly planted on his body.

They re-enact the scene. The empowerment of the female in the new configuration is immediately evident.

Re-enactments can be initiated scene by scene, or subsequent to discussion.

Future projection

Students are asked to write their FF characters' hopes and dreams for the future for presentation to the group. The FF future scenes (10 years in the future) provide opportunity for significant changes in attitudes and behaviours on the part of the fictional family members. If they wish, they can resolve their characters' personal and/or social issues, and share an "ending" with the larger group.

Socialization

The behaviours of individuals outside their families is often markedly different from their communication styles at home: likewise with the characters in the fictional families. Therefore actors are encouraged to interact with characters from outside fictional families (Cross-Family Conflicts). Designed to further explore the possibly suppressed or stifled dimensions of the FF characters' personalities, these scenes give those students who might have simply replicated their own biases and/or reproduced politically correct stances, to 'come out' with opposite points of view furthering awareness and opportunity for discussion.

Fictional Family Group Encounter

A second example of cross-family scenes is the FF group encounter. Modelled on a real-life therapy group, the encounter session which I direct is designed to offer the fictional family characters an opportunity to listen to, and interact with, another fictional family who also has communication problems. In a class focused on gender these problems will be centred on gender issues. The encounter provides the actors with an opportunity to develop new choices in communication style for their characters in future FF scenes and gives them an opportunity to maintain their FF roles throughout an entire session.

1. The students are asked whether they wish to have a FF therapy session. The session is carried out only if there is a great deal of interest and enthusiasm. It is also suggested that the session be tape recorded in case they wish to listen to the exchange of dialogue at some future time. Listening to the tape can serve as the basis for future discussion and or performance.

2. The students enter the room as their FF characters and immediately sit in a circle ready for the session to begin. There is absolute quiet. After a few moments, I, as leader, open the group encounter session. I suggest that they have all come here because they have communication problems with members of their fictional families and that their presence indicates that they hope to change and improve these relationships. I tell them that everything that will be said here should be considered confidential.

3. My role as "therapist" is non-confrontational. I intervene as little as possible, and the tone of the intervention, whether in question or statement form, is gentle, supportive and/or neutral.

4. All four fictional families are simultaneously involved in the session. Therefore, if a FF member wishes to make a confidential statement to the outside families, h/er family is requested to "freeze" during those specific moments. This *'behind the back'* technique borrowed from psychodrama allows FF members to uninterruptedly and freely express their feelings about other family members; it additionally gives input to those family members who are 'physically' absent.

5. FF members commence with a statement which expresses their objectives. They state what it is they want, need and hope for themselves and their fictional families. They attempt to articulate what they want to change in order to achieve the desired state of coming to understand and trust one another. This technique ties in with family therapy strategies where families are assisted in finding new possibilities for communication so that they can function more effectively.

6. Closure. The FF characters are asked to express a mood or feeling through movement and/or words-and a hope for the future. The actors are then requested to relinquish their FF roles and relate to the experience from the actor's perspective. As in all other processes, they write of their experience in their *journals* and *character diaries*. I cite here an example of a FF group encounter session in which several of the dramatic techniques described above were used.

Fictional Family members of both families were seated in one large circle. The Ferris family was embroiled in an issue focusing on their mother, Gillian, who had disclosed as her secret the fact that she planned to go to Europe for a year to write a book. Feelings of rejection, abandonment and anger were expressed by her FF members. However, they had difficulty expressing their emotions directly to her. During the session, her husband, Wilfred expressed his anxiety that she would not return to the family and his need to know her plans. Gillian continued to be non-committal. Wilfred was coaxed to ask her directly for a commitment.

Finally, the discussion became focused on Mandy, the youngest child's need for her mother to be with her. Mandy had considerable difficulty expressing her needs to her mother. Eventually, following considerable *'side coaching'*, Mandy went over to her mother to beg her to stay. Since Gillian was unable to give the commitment the family needed, Susie, Mandy's older sister, was requested to speak *('double')* for her mother. She said that she (representing Gillian) was not planning to return to her family. Gillian concurred.

The group was then asked to play a *tug of war* with an imaginary rope in which those who empathized with Gillian, the mother, would pull the rope on her side, and those on the side of Mandy, her daughter, would pull on the opposite side. The rope was heavily weighted on Mandy's side. Subsequent to the game, in *post-performance discussion*, the group observed that mothers in general have little support.

Post-Performance Discussion

Discussion can take place following each fictional family's performance. Or, one can wait until all the fictional families have performed. In the latter model, one has the opportunity to contrast and compare the varied attitudes, behaviours, issues, resolutions, and the effectiveness of the theatrical presentations.

Research Papers

A research paper on the topic of Divorce was described earlier in this chapter in which a student initiated this topic after observing the fictional families in a variety of scenes. Next she did some reading up on the topic, after which she developed a list of interview questions which she posed to the fictional families. And finally she researched further to see whether the responses corroborated the research findings.

In a sociology or social studies class, the teacher might supply students with a pertinent reading list. She could also furnish them with a questionnaire and ask them to interview members of a 'real' family. The student can present her findings to the class for class input and discussion, or start the research before the fictional families are even formed. Some fictional families might then be modelled on case studies encountered in the research process.

Summary

The FF technique, although designed for actor training, can work as a powerful tool to create awareness in its participants of gender discrimination, sexual stereotyping, and traditional perspectives of women as lesser contributors to a variety of cultures and fields. Through dramatic enactment of their characters' lives, societal attitudes and behaviours are clearly reflected, giving teachers an ideal opportunity to underline the connections between these attitudes and behaviours. By seizing this opportunity, they can facilitate the group's sensitivity to, and awareness of, the possibility of effecting change.

There has been no attempt here to provide teachers with lesson plans. They are the experts in their own particular disciplines. The intention is rather to hope to inspire them to incorporate FF with their particular subjects.

References

Bassnett-McGuire, Susan E. Towards a Theory of Women's Theatre. *Semiotics of Drama and Theatre: New Perspectives on the Theory of Drama and Theatre*, (Ed.). Herta Schmid and Alysius Van Kestern. Amsterdam: John Benjamins, 1984

Blair, Rhonda. Liberating the Young Actor: Feminist Pedagogy and Performance. *Theatre Topics,* Vol. 2, No.1, 1992.

Case, Sue-Ellen. *Feminism and Theatre.* London, MacMillan, 1988.

Davis, Tracy C. *A Doll's House and the Evolving Feminist Agenda: A Feminist Research Prospect and Retrospect.* ed. Peta Tancred-Sheriff. McGill Queen's University Press, 1988.

Dell, Paul F. Violence and the Systemic View: The Problem of Power. *Family Process,* Vol. 28, No.1, 1-14. Family Process, Inc., 1989.

Dolan, Jill. *The Feminist Spectator as Critic.* Ann Arbor. UMI, 1988.

Ellis, Mary Lynne. Women: The Mirage of the Perfect Image. *The Arts in Psychotherapy.* Vol. 16, No.4, 263-276. Pergamon Press, 1989.

Gold, Muriel. *The Fictional Family: In Drama, Education and Groupwork.* Springfield: Charles C Thomas, 1991.

Gold, Muriel. *Therapy Through Drama: The Fictional Family,* Springfield: Charles C Thomas, 2000.

Jent, Deanna Banz. *Sex Roles in the Acting Class: Exploring the Effects of Actor Training on Nonverbal Gender Display,* Doctoral dissertation, Evanston: 1989.

Laird, Joan. Women and Ritual in Family Therapy. *In* Evan Imber-Black, Janine Roberts and Richard Whiting (Eds.). *Rituals in Families and Family Therapy.* New York: W. W. Norton & Company, 1988.

McGoldrick, Monica and Elizabeth A. Carter. The Family Life Cycle. *In* Froma Walsh (Ed.). *Normal Family Processes.* New York: The Guilford Press, 1982.

Price, Sharon and Patrick McHenry. *Divorce.* Sage, 1988.

Siegel, Marilyn. *Exploratory Study of the Long-Tern Unattached* unpublished doctoral thesis, McGill University, Montreal,1989.

Strongylu, Nina. Cultural Identity & Gender. *Dramascope*, Vol. X, No. 1, 9-10, 1990.

Todd, Susan. *Women & Theatre: Calling the Shots.* London: Faber & Faber, 1984.

Walsh, Froma. The family in later life. *In* E.A. Carter & M. McGoldrick (Eds.). *The family life cycle: A framework for family therapy.* New York: Gardner Press, 1980.

Wilcoxon, S. Allen. Contemporary Developments in Marital and Family Therapy. *Family Therapy,* Vol. XVI, No.1, 87-94 San Diego: Libra Publishers, Inc., 1989

Chapter Nine:

Integrating the Fictional Family Technique into Planning for Teaching

David Dillon

In this volume you have been introduced to the Fictional Family (FF) technique itself, have encountered a rationale for the use of improvised drama as a learning medium across the curriculum, and have reviewed a number of descriptions of the FF technique in applied use in various teaching contexts and for various learning purposes. This chapter looks ahead to imagine new possibilities for the use of the technique across the curriculum. It is designed to explore in some detail the process of planning for the use of the FF technique as part of one's own teaching. After considering some general principles, I share several examples of my own relatively detailed instructional plans for the use of the FF technique in several different areas of the curriculum which attempt to follow those general principles. The purpose in this approach is not to try to provide plans which other teachers can necessarily "pick up" and use. There is too much variation in content and teaching approach among the readers of this volume to even consider such a goal. Rather, my hope is that my own examples, both as a process and a product, might serve as helpful transitions to your own planning for teaching, based on your own particular content and your own students.

Muriel Gold, C.M., Ph.D.

General Principles

Before looking at several specific examples of my own planning from various subject areas, there are several general considerations that apply broadly to the use of improvisational drama in general and the FF technique in particular in planning for teaching.

Where Does Drama Fit Within a Unit of Inquiry?

I view improvisational drama techniques, FF or others, as one tool among many at a teacher's disposal to help foster learning. Thus, it is normally used in conjunction with the usual uses of reading, explanations, discussion, written assignments, and even tests to help students learn and normally requires little change in those other teaching and learning techniques. In my examples that follow later in this chapter, therefore, I focus only on the possible use of the FF technique for a particular topic. Other teaching steps would need to be taken in any unit of inquiry, but I make no attempt to suggest what they should be since there is already great variation in teaching techniques among different teachers. It is up to each reader to decide where these techniques might best fit in their current teaching plans. I might add that while the focus in the following plans is on the improvisational drama activities themselves, it is almost always helpful, if not important, to allow students to discuss insights revealed through any of the improvisations immediately following the drama activities.

In addition, there is no "right" answer for where drama might best fit within an inquiry. Much depends on a teacher's intentions for its use. Some teachers occasionally will use drama fairly early in a unit of inquiry in order to see what students already know about a topic—whether accurate or not, extensive or limited. (And students will almost always know *something* about a topic!) Such early use of the technique allows teachers to assess students' current understanding and to plan better for subsequent instruction. Many teachers, however, will tend to use drama later in a unit of inquiry in order to allow students to put into "action" and "extend" much of the conceptual learning they have been engaged in about the topic to that point. Finally, placing drama at some mid-point in an inquiry allows both intentions to be at work to some extent.

How Does One Adjust the FF Technique for Subject Matter Learning?

In a drama education course, there is enormous "space" for learners to create their families, their individual characters, and the conflicts they will encounter since it is the processes of improvising, character development, and so on that are the focus of such a course. In other curriculum areas, however, a teacher needs to determine more "givens" for most uses of the technique as a learning medium for particular content. In general, I see two kinds of contexts that subject-area teachers often need to provide for students in using the FF technique. One is often greater determination of who the families will be and what the issues are that will cause conflict and tension in the improvising. Second, is that a teacher must often determine the larger socio-cultural context in which the family will be improvising and often decide that it is larger social events, times, and trends that will impact on family dynamics. Teachers need not hesitate to set these frameworks and limits. There will still be much "space" within the predetermined frameworks for students' creative improvisation and discovery.

How Does One Apply the FF Technique in Subject Matter Teaching?

As Gold describes in an earlier chapter in this volume, the FF technique is made up of a number of different kind of scenes for improvisation. In a drama education course, most or all of them would be done in a certain order. In using the technique for subject matter learning, however, a teacher would normally pick and choose which kinds of scenes or activities might help achieve particular instructional goals. Thus, if a teacher wants students to understand what a character in a novel is like, then some of the activities that focus more on character development might be appropriate, *e.g., Your FF Character: A Past Incident.* If the goal is understanding the basic theme or conflict of an historical time or event, then an activity that focuses on conflict will help, *e.g., The FF in Crisis.* If a teacher feels that understanding or anticipating the long-term consequences of particular decisions is important, then perhaps *The FF 10 Years in the Future* would be an appropriate activity. Or if families' socioeconomic situations might be important for students' understanding, then the activity on *FF Houses* might help. In short, subject area teachers normally use only a few of the FF activities at any one time and they choose those activities which will help achieve their learning goals for students.

What Kind of Learning is Improvised Drama Good For?

The essence of drama is dramatic tension around a clash of wills or needs of different characters. This tension provides a focus for the drama and causes it to "move" forward and unfold somehow toward a resolution. The tension or conflict exists at two levels. One is the specific, concrete level of the actual problem in this story. (For example, should Romeo and Juliet elope, defying their families?) The other is the more general or universal human issue or dilemma which that one particular problem represents. (For example, the sense of belonging, identity, and loyalty to one's family and social group versus one's individuality and responsibility to oneself, or the tension between what our heart wants for us *versus* what others want from us for their own needs.) Both levels always exist simultaneously. While there are many, many different specific problems that appear in stories, there tend to be fewer of the universal issues in stories and they appear again and again in various guises in different stories. In the same way, while there are uncountable specific characters in stories, there are far fewer character types that appear again and again—good and bad, perpetrator and victim, madonna and whore, powerful and weak, and so on. In fact, in the field of family counselling, many authors describe family dynamics in terms of a relatively small number of "scripts" and "roles" that we learn to play—and become.

The importance of these principles is twofold. One is that it is the general or universal theme that often allows students to find a personal link with the topic under study. For example, any students who have felt pressure from those with power over them to make certain decisions or behave in a certain way may be able to relate to and understand Romeo and Juliet's feelings and the nature of the dilemma they face.

Secondly, it means that teachers must apply improvisational drama to those same kinds of universal human themes and dilemmas in their own subject areas. In other words, drama is best for helping students see and explore the bigger human issues that we all share in and live. In practice, this may mean focusing on the main themes and issues in literature, the larger themes and trends in history or economics, the dilemmas and struggles caused by technological development, and so on in one's teaching and using drama to help expose them and help students understand them. Furthermore, it means that drama's main focus should not be practicing to get facts or processes right. Those aspects are certainly important in any subject area and specific information and skills are always present in stories, but they are always secondary to the tension and conflict among characters. Thus, during improvisations students may sometimes reveal certain misunderstandings or gaps in their knowledge. However, it is generally best to deal with those aspects outside the drama, perhaps in a follow-up discussion or a future lesson, so as not to interfere with or even distort the nature of the dramatic experience.

Dorothy Heathcote (1971) once explained this key point in a striking way as part of a television program on her pioneering work in drama in education. She had worked with a group of students to help them create a drama on their suggested topic of a prisoner-of-war camp set in World War II. The main problem the group introduced into the drama was the planting of a German stool pigeon to spy among the British prisoners. In helping the student playing the stool pigeon understand the demands of the task and prepare for it, Heathcote was helping him build a false British background. When she asked him where he was from in England, he said he was from Coventry, in London. Heathcote made no attempt to correct him and moved on with the task. (Coventry is a city approximately 150 kilometres north of London.) After the drama session, the television interviewer asked her why she didn't tell the boy that Coventry was not in London. Heathcote replied:

> Because I don't give a damn where Coventry is! At that point he *felt* right. He was working on an intensity of feeling, not on facts at all. I was saying, "You've got to convince Englishmen!" and he said "Yes!" And *that's* the level we're working at. If he'd said "The Man in the Moon," as long as he'd believed it at that point, it's OK by me. After all, what's a fact? I just happen to know that Coventry isn't in London, but there's loads of things I could have said equally stupid if you're looking at this kind of stupidity. If the other boys, of course, had suddenly jeered at him, I would have had to defend him. But nobody jeered because it was as right for them because they were feeling as well. I think that this is something that is very, very delicate. Sometimes one would have to say, "Are you sure?" But I . . . (shakes her head). This knowing what's irrelevant is the most important thing there is in teaching!

The Nature of Planning for Teaching

Finally, teaching is a complex human activity and, by its very nature, very difficult to completely predetermine or control. Yet we must still plan for our teaching in some way. The specific plans that follow are based on a sense of direction and some larger steps to consider in moving toward that goal. Yet, I have tried to stop short of predetermining the activities in a rigid and highly prescribed manner. A teacher must determine so much on how initial steps go, by gauging needs and interests in a group, and adjusting subsequent steps in a plan accordingly. Therefore, I have attempted to create a "moderate" framework of a plan, with room for decisions and choices at various points depending on the nature of the group, the time and interest available, and so on.

Let's move on and look at more specific plans for several topics from various areas of the curriculum--English, Science and Technology, and Social Studies.

English

While definitions of "English" certainly vary and the field is increasingly undergoing redefinition, two aspects seem to remain anchored in what is referred to as "English": literature and creative writing. The staying power of these aspects may be due in large part as well to the fact that other disciplines tend not to include them, so that English remains their only home.

The FF technique can be used as a means of helping students understand more deeply and insightfully, especially in a "felt" way, the nature of characters in a story and the human issues that lie between them. It can also help foster students' own personal interpretation and response to the story and its issues. Adding creative writing to the drama techniques can help as well to foster students' personal response to a story.

Improvised drama means that scenes are contextualized and framed at some starting point, but that outcomes are not predetermined. Outcomes are determined only in the actual playing out of the scene. For that reason, it is usually preferable to create scenes that have <u>not</u> actually happened in the original story, since students may tend to have the scene turn out the way it does in the story. Rather, it is usually preferable to create scenes "around" the original story, scenes that are not in the story but which conceivably could have happened. Ideally, these scenes will help evoke and elicit the key aspects of characters as well as the central issues and dilemmas in stories.

As an example, let's consider *Romeo and Juliet*. It is a text that is commonly studied and, indeed, is part of popular culture. For our purposes it is helpful that readers already know the story very well. In addition, this play provides an interesting and obvious "way into" the use of FF technique since the role of family plays such an important part in the story. Some initial framing of the families is provided in the play, but much is left implied and few scenes in the play actually deal with family dynamics, though much is suggested. In short, a rich possibility for the FF technique. The main goals in using the technique are to help readers understand the main characters better and particularly to understand the nature of the issues and dilemmas they face.

Preliminary steps

Assign roughly equal numbers of groups of students to create either the Montague or the Capulet family, feeling free to use not only actual characters from the play, but to also create additional family members, close or extended, who would be feasible or realistic. *(This choice provides the possibility for students to consider the story's main dispute from both sides and to explore both differences and similarities between the two sides. By creating several "versions" of each family, it also creates the possibility of diverse perspectives and responses to each family situation, a "plural" or "kaleidoscopic" view that should enrich group meaning-making with the text and diversity of personal response to it.)*

Using whatever they know about the family, the context of the story, the historical times, and so on, groups take turns showing their FF at a meal in order to introduce the members of the family and to provide some background on them, the context of the family, *etc*. If necessary or helpful, spend some time helping the class brainstorm possibilities for various family members to include, what might be the nature of the discussion at meals at that time, and so on.

Character and Context Development

Depending on the time available and the students' willingness, it may be helpful to spend a bit of time helping students develop their characters and the problematic situation of the story. Two FF steps seem appropriate for this purpose and one or both may be done.

Your Fictional Character: A Past Incident. Each member of each FF group decides on a past incident that may have shaped them very much the way they are today. They then "perform" this incident. (If time allows, each student can perform for the whole class. If not, each character can perform for their own fictional family.) The performance will often be a monologue recounting the particular event and the character's reactions and feelings. It may involve some improvised dialogue on their part to help bring the event to life. *(Such a dramatic and oral crafting of an event is often an excellent preparation for creative writing in which the event and the characters' reactions and thoughts become the basis for fictional prose, poetry, or even a script for a dramatic performance.)*

Your Fictional Family 10 Years Ago. Each group decides on a scene for the family 10 years earlier that would reveal some of the roots of the family dynamics today, but also perhaps some of the changes and differences that might have occurred over time. While each group will have to make some decisions about the situation to portray generally, much of the playing

187

should still be improvisational within the general framework decided on. Each "family" performs its scene for the rest of the class.

Conflict

Exploring the conflict or main tension in a story would be centrally important to understanding and relating to a literary text. Thus several FF activities would lend themselves to this goal and would be the heart of the use of the FF technique in this situation:

The Fictional Family Faces a Crisis. Each group decides what internal conflict might arise for their family, particularly one that would be centrally related to the story. For example, actual events from the story could be used as the prompts for crisis: Tibalt's death at the hands of Mercutio or even the deaths of Romeo and Juliet themselves could cause internal dissension within a family about how to respond, who is at fault, *etc.* On the other hand, groups could create a new, yet probable, crisis that would reveal more about each of the family members and the dynamics among them. Each group improvises their crisis for the whole class.

Your Character's Secret Creates Family Conflict. Various members of each family can decide on a secret to reveal to the family, a secret that will cause tension and crisis within the family. Once again, the secrets could be based on events in the actual play such as Romeo or Juliet revealing to their family their love of the other and their desire to marry, deciding to try to convince their family to agree to the marriage and to stop feuding. Or, other secrets could be invented for revelation, for example, a male character's revelation that he is too afraid to engage in a real fight with the other family, someone's revelation that they are not in agreement with the feud and will not support it, or a character's desire to break from the family for some reason thus threatening its solidarity. If time allows, each revelation of a secret could be improvised for the whole class. Otherwise, each group can improvise its various revelations just for itself.

Cross-family Conflict. Assign students in pairs to work with a member of another family group, but always in a Capulet-Montague pairing. These pairs decide how their characters might encounter each other and what tension might arise from that. They then improvise that scene. There may well be too many scenes to show to the whole class, but a selection of some could be shown or the results and insights across the class could certainly be surveyed and discussed after the improvisations. *(Such a scene not only allows further development of each character through improvising in a new context, but ideally it would enrich and broaden the class's understanding of the nature of the tension in the story and its multiple ramifications. It also adds interest and variety to students' work as they have a chance to improvise with new partners after several improvisations within their own group.)*

Consequences

A key aspect of literature is that our actions have consequences. They may shape our futures in very determining ways or characters may be able to make choices about how they respond to circumstances. If a teacher or class would be interested in exploring this aspect of the story, one particular FF activity seems most appropriate:

The FF 10 Years in the Future. Each group decides on a particular scene 10 years in the future that will allow them to explore and reveal the effects of the deaths of Romeo and Juliet on them some time later, as well as the meaning they have made of this tragic event for themselves. Each group performs its improvisation for the whole class.

Final Notes

The possibility of having students engage in personal or creative writing as a way of responding further to the story exists at many points throughout this developmental sequence or it could be done after the dramatizing has been completed. A number of kinds of writing are possible. Students could simply write about their own personal insights and reactions to the story afforded by the improvising in a sort of "personal response to literature" journal. On the other hand they could write reflections or poetry as either themselves or as the character they are playing. Finally, students could use their improvisations as the base to experiment with various genres, to recreate what they improvised, for example, in script form, in fictional narrative prose, or in poetic form. Ideally, students' writing would be shared and discussed in class for insights to not only the story, but also to writing as both process and product.

In addition, the approach described here for literature (and writing) could apply in the same general ways for historical events. The terms "story" and "history" share the same etymological root (the French word *l'histoire*) and would benefit from similar uses of the FF technique.

Science and Technology

These two formerly separate fields are being increasing linked in curriculum revisions in light of the increasing awareness that it is the technological application of basic scientific principles that affects our daily lives for better or for worse and creates issues and tensions among people. This shift opens possibilities for the use of drama as a learning medium in this area of the curriculum since drama is about issues that lie between people—not between cells, molecules, or vectors.

Technological applications of scientific principles and facts have been a two-edged sword, contributing enormously to the quality of life in our society, but also creating enormous problems for our society at the same time. For example, the development of the internal combustion engine and the automobile has enhanced transportation possibilities for us, but has also created a host of problems from noise, poor air quality, and urban sprawl to global warming and the depletion of vital energy resources of the planet. The development of many medical procedures has saved and enhanced lives, but has also created enormous ethical and moral dilemmas such as issues around keeping individuals alive, surrogate motherhood, and cloning. Mechanical and chemical developments have made farming more cost efficient and productive, but have also raised questions about the effect on our health and the elimination of the family farm in favour of huge international corporations that control food production.

This list would be easy to extend at some length. The important fact is how these developments create issues for individuals and for us as a society, issues that result in tensions among people that must be resolved. Drama situations can help explore not just basic scientific facts and principles, but the issues that their applications create for us humans.

As one example to develop in this curricular area, let's consider principles of ecology (i.e., the interconnected nature of all life on earth, including humans, and the repercussions of harming that delicate balance through human activity). Within this framework, we include not only our effect as humans on the planet's ecological health (*e.g.*, pollution, disappearance of species of flora and fauna, *etc.*), but also the effect of these changes on us (smog alerts that cause people to stay indoors, depletion of the ozone layer that causes increased risk of skin cancer, agricultural approaches that contaminate ground water and our food, *etc.*).

In addition, of course, families and society are peopled by a wide range of different approaches and perspectives that individuals take to this issue, from those who believe it is mankind's right to dominate and exploit nature to those who work actively to promote more environmentally-friendly ways of living. Such diversity also causes tensions, e.g., between large corporations and Greenpeace.

Drama always deals in very specific and particular examples. Thus, basing drama activities on ecological issues usually means looking at very specific and localized examples of these larger issues, that is, the causes and effects of one family's activity on the planet's ecology, as well as local social issues on environmental concerns.

Preliminary steps

Review with students many of the specific ways that our lifestyles have environmental effects. Some examples include the amount of energy used (electric, natural gas, gasoline, *etc.*), the amount of resources used (packaging of products, disposable cups, plates, and cutlery at fast food restaurants, water, *etc.*), pollution (household cleaning products, amount of driving, disposing of non-biodegradable materials, *etc.*), and so on.

Review also with students the range of stances that people take toward their environmental responsibility, from negligent to responsible, from uninvolved to activist, using as many actual examples as possible.

Ask students to form family groups which will include different stances towards ecological concerns and in which ecological concerns will form the basis of dramatic tension. For example, the ecological concerns might involve the amount of use of natural resources (leaving lights on when no one is in a room, taking long showers with hot water, taking unnecessary trips in the car or deciding about buying a gas guzzler or a second car versus using public transport), damaging pollution (using toxic domestic cleaning products which are cheaper versus using biodegradable products that are more expensive and not as easily accessible, buying products with extensive and wasteful packaging versus bulk buying, or patronizing fast food restaurants that use large amounts of disposable materials, the use of CFCs in air conditioners or aerosols), and so on.

All of these issues can cause conflict and tension in a family since these decisions impinge on individual's comfort, pleasure, freedom, money, and lifestyle generally. Students would also need to decide on different stances toward these issues on the part of members of the family in order for there to be tension and conflict around family decisions. For example, a young, idealistic son launches a crusade at home to have his family live in a more environmentally friendly way and members of his family have a range of reactions to his pressure.

Each group improvises for the rest of the class a breakfast scene which will reveal the conflicts and the various dynamics among family members over them. *(Note that dynamics among family members due to personality and past history-e.g., sibling rivalry, intergenerational conflict, etc.-may well interweave with conflicts over ecological concerns since human relations are complex and that complexity often shows in improvised scenes.)*

Character and Context Development

It may be not only helpful, but also important, for individual family members to explore what may be some of the origins and roots of their beliefs and perspectives on environmental concerns and to see what differences exist among people in this regard. Just as important as what the environmental issues are may be how we are influenced to understand and act in various ways, and even whether or not we are aware of that influence.

Your FF Character: A Past Incident. Each family member creates a past incident that will help explain how and why she or he thinks and feels as they do today. It may be a matter of being inspired by an environmental activist, of encountering someone with a deeply ecological and spiritual view of humankind's harmony with nature, being shocked at the results of environmental studies, being influenced—one way or the other—by advertising, wanting to be like someone else the character admires, just going along with "normal" living in our society, and so on. There may not be time to perform all the individual characters' past incidents, but each should be performed at least within each family group and perhaps surveyed and discussed as a whole group afterward.

Conflict

Playing out various conflicts over environmental issues in the family groups should sensitize students to the actual ecological issues they live hour to hour and perhaps even minute to minute as they decide their way through their day (thus linking course content on scientific principles to their lived experience). It should also help reveal the complexity and difficulty of the various dilemmas surrounding these issues, even on the small scale of one family. Several FF techniques are applicable here:

The FF in Conflict: Pairs. Members of a family pair up and decide on an environmental conflict to improvise. The improvised scenes should be shown to at least their family groups. If time and interest allow, most or all could be shown to the whole class as well as discussed. *(Note that this activity not only exposes a particular conflict, but also continues to help develop each of the characters through their engaging in conflict with another.)*

The FF Faces a Crisis. Each group creates a major conflict which engages the whole family and plays out the scene for the whole group.

Cross-family Conflict: Pairs. Arrange for pairs from among the various family groups to encounter each other, trying to arrange for different perspectives and stances on issues. Students in each pair decide how they might encounter each other and what issue might arise. They then improvise the scene. Survey the results afterward with the whole class. *(While a major focus of this plan is for students to link school knowledge with their lifestyles at home, the value of an activity like this one is that it can extend the applicability of ecological principles—and our responsibility around them—beyond the immediate family and the home to a broader social arena.)*

Consequences

Since a major reason for learning about ecological principles and environmental issues is society's concern about looming problems for the future, it seems important to explore the consequences of the decisions made by various families, not only for themselves but also for the planet and for society.

The Fictional Family 10 Years in the Future. Each group imagines their family 10 years in the future after the previous family conflict scene and improvises the scene for the rest of the class. (*Note that such a scene reveals not only the consequences for that particular family, but also should provide a backdrop on where humankind has come to in terms of the environment in the future. Students need to imagine and logically extend the consequences of decisions that may have seemed short-term at first.*)

Final Notes

This plan chose to focus on highly localized issues within a home and family context. The techniques could also be used to deal with environmental issues on a larger social scale—decisions about garbage dumps, municipal by-laws about garbage, pesticides, *etc.*, involvement in activist causes and educational campaigns, and so on—all of which can create conflict within a family.

Social Studies

The field of social studies includes a broad range of sub-areas (which become increasingly specialized later in the education system): history, geography, economics, sociology, anthropology, *etc.* The use of drama as a learning medium seems most applicable to the area of history since it is made of up various characters, specific events, larger themes and issues, *etc.*—all very "dramatic" in nature. However, even the other aspects of social studies can lend themselves to the use of drama as a learning medium. The key notion is that basic facts, general principles, *etc.* from a discipline must be placed within an actual and specific context of human interaction and conflict, in this case family life. I would like to propose the use of economics, and to some extent geography, as the basis for this illustration, to help explain the application of drama in these areas.

One of the basic aims of economics education is to explore the interrelated aspects and the cause-and-effect dynamics of the various components of any economic system, *e.g.*, the dynamic of supply and demand and its effect on the cost of goods and services in a capitalist system or the role and intervention of government in any economic system.

The nature of our economic system has changed dramatically in recent decades as a global economy has developed rapidly around the world. It is no longer possible to consider any economy in local terms. Most of the key aspects of our lives are part of a complex and highly interrelated web. Much of the food and clothing we buy is produced elsewhere (beef in Brazil, clothing in China, sports equipment in Pakistan), jobs not only shift quickly in nature in today's economy, but also shift location quickly as large multinational corporations continually seek the most favourable conditions in a competitive world (leading for example, to large shifts of where jobs are created or lost), our economy has become more of an information- and service-based economy (as opposed to traditional manufactured goods), standards for environmental protection, worker safety, unionization, *etc.,* have suffered in this internationally competitive environment, the power of governments has been diminished in the face of increasingly large and powerful corporations, reducing government more to the role of handmaiden for business and less as a regulatory role for business. The list of shifts could be extended, but just this partial listing may provide some hint of the profound effect of these recent shifts on individual families, here in Canada but also in other countries. This enormous change means not only that students must understand the basics of this shift in the economy of which we are a part, but they must also develop a global awareness and a sense of global responsibility as Canadian workers and consumers.

With that goal in mind, the following use of the FF technique is designed to help build understanding of globalization as well as building sensitivity and awareness of the highly interrelated world we live in.

Preliminary steps

Review with students a number of the ordinary, taken-for-granted aspects of their daily lives that have impact on people far away. For example, the hamburger they eat at a fast-food restaurant may come from cattle raised in Brazil and the tomato on it may have been raised in Mexico (particularly during our winter), much of the clothing they buy (and are currently wearing!) has usually been made by women in southeast Asia, the soccer ball they kick at lunchtime or after school may have been manufactured in Pakistan by children younger than themselves.

Economics Education

Consider as well the advantages and disadvantages of each situation for local families. For example, North American demand for beef developed a large industry in Brazil, but also destroyed much of the rain forest—with a big effect on climate change. Much agricultural production around the world creates jobs as well, but workers often suffer from contact with harmful pesticides and fertilizers which are not tightly regulated in those countries. Clothing or sports equipment manufacturing also creates employment in many countries, but work days tend to be long and wages very low. As well, work demands can interfere with family life, children's education, and so on. The development of a tourist industry in Cuba created jobs within a sustainable economy and brought hard currency into a poor country, but has created undesirable social stresses as bus boys at tourist hotels now often earn much more than doctors, engineers, or teachers.

Depending on the examples used in the first steps (and the background information available to students), choose certain family situations that will relate to those examples. For example, families in Brazil, Mexico, China, Pakistan, *etc.*, as well, of course, as in Canada. Have several of the groups play different kinds of Canadian families. Decide as well on possible conflicts that could arise in these families due to global economic factors, *e.g.*, a child in a family considering stopping school in order to work in a factory, a father suffering from exposure to chemicals in his agricultural work, a mother's long days in a clothing factory that take her away from her family responsibilities, families (including Canadian ones) disrupted because of father and/or mother losing jobs as their companies relocate, and so on.

Have each group improvise for the rest of the class a scene at breakfast that will introduce the characters and the situation in which they are economically.

Character and Context Development
Several possible FF activities would apply at this stage of the inquiry.

FF Houses. Each group creates a pictorial representation of their home to share with the rest of the class. *(Note that this activity should help students consider more carefully the socioeconomic status and situation of their fictional families and create possibilities for comparison with a Canadian situation.)*

The FF Faces a Crisis. Each group decides on an economically related conflict which they improvise and show to the rest of the class.

The FF 10 Years Ago. Each group decides on an earlier incident to improvise as a family, one that will reveal as much as possible some of the antecedents and possible roots of the current crisis. *(Note that such an activity may open possibilities for students to consider whether families are actually better off today than they were 10 years ago—has the economic change been an improvement or not?)*

Conflict

Your Character's Secret Creates Family Conflict. Each group improvises one or more secrets revealed by family members that cause conflict, especially that may threaten the economic stability of the family, e.g. a child's desire to stay in school rather than work, a mother's desire to stay at home rather than work, a father's desire to try a less stable job but one he may enjoy more, *etc. (Such an activity may help reveal the tight economic web that many families find themselves in and how limited some of their choices in life may be because of economic systems.)*

Cross-family Conflicts: Pairs. Create situations in which one member of a Canadian family encounters a member of a family from another country. Possible situations could include going on vacation to that country, being in that country to conduct business, meeting at a conference on a theme of mutual interest (such as an international youth conference), and so on. Decide on a possible source of conflict and improvise it, if not for the whole class at least for the two family groups involved. (This activity would be very important to help expose some of the interrelated issues we all share globally, but also some of the different perceptions and understandings of them.)

Consequences

The FF 10 Years in the Future. Each family group improvises for the rest of the class a key scene 10 years in the future based on the outcome of the original crises they faced as a family. *(I stress the importance of this activity for the purpose of having students consider not only the consequences of particular decisions for a family, but also to infer and imagine the future implications of today's current economic situation for families in various parts of our global economic system.)*

Looking Ahead

The purpose of this chapter has been to explain and illustrate the integration of the tool of FF technique into the process of planning for teaching in various subject areas. Its hope is to enable readers to see more clearly the possible uses of the technique in their own teaching and how they might take some initial steps in that direction. You may have used other improvisational dramatic techniques in your teaching and the possible incorporation of this technique may feel like a relatively small and quite do-able step. On the other hand, if you have not used drama as a learning medium before, the use of this technique may seem like a big-and uncertain-step. If so, it is only natural to feel some hesitation, even anxiety.

I work with many teacher education students in courses on drama in education. Few students have had much experience with drama prior to the course and often take big steps personally as I lead drama sessions with them or they lead sessions with each other in the course. Usually they are quite positive and enthusiastic about their experiences in the course. However, they tend to feel quite hesitant and anxious about using drama with students in classrooms. Their concerns usually include:

fear either that learners will not have the ability to improvise because it is too advanced a skill for them

concern that students may view drama as a childish activity and thus see the teacher in a reduced light for engaging in it

fear that they will lose control of the class as students do "whatever they want".

Just as striking as is the uniformity of teachers' concerns *prior* to using drama with their students is the uniformity of their reactions *after* trying drama as part of their teaching. Generally, they note:

how powerful and interesting the technique was for students' learning, often generating great interest, widespread involvement, and effective learning

how the technique revealed dimensions and abilities of their students they had not seen before (often including positive aspects of students that had not been previously involved)

how the use of drama enhanced teachers' relations with students, making them healthier as teacher and student relate differently and effectively with each other.

Perhaps the best summary comes from a student teacher who used improvisational drama for the first time in conjunction with her class's study of a novel and e-mailed me that very day to tell me that she was "giddy with delight" at the result.

You may well feel convinced of the benefits of drama as a learning medium. I hope this chapter might help you develop some of the skills and understandings for using it in your own teaching.

References

Gold, Muriel. *THE FICTIONAL FAMILY In Drama, Education and Groupwork.* Springfield, Ill. Charles C Thomas, 1991

Heathcote, Dorothy. *"Three Looms Waiting."* BBC Television production, 1971.

General Bibliography

Appel, Libby. *Mask Characterization: An Acting Process.* Carbondale. Southern Illinois University Press, 1982

Bandler, Richard, John Grinder and Virginia Satir. *Changing With Families.* Palo Alto. Science and Behavior Books Inc., 1976

Barnes, Douglas. *From Communication to Curriculum (2nd editions).* Portsmouth, NH: Boynton/Cook, Heinemann, 1992.

Barnes, Douglas, James Britton, Mike Torbe. *Language, the Learner and the School.* Portsmouth, N.H.: Boynton/Cook, 1990.

Barr, Mary and Mary K. Healy. "Language Across the Curriculum." *Handbook of Research on Teaching the English Language Arts.* Ed. James Flood et al. London: Macmillan, 1991.

Barrs, Myra. "Voice and Role in Reading and Writing." *Language Arts,* 64, 2: 207-218, 1987.

Barton, Robert. *Acting Onstage and off.* (4th ed.) Belmont, CA. Thomson Wadsworth, 2006.

Bassnett-McGuire, Susan E. "Towards a Theory of Women's Theatre." *Semiotics of Drama and Theatre: New Perspectives on the Theory of Drama and Theatre,* (Ed.). Herta Schmid and Alysius Van Kestern. Amsterdam: John Benjamins, 1984

Benedetti, Robert: *The Actor at Work.* Englewood Cliffs, N.J. Prentice Hall, 1970.

Muriel Gold, C.M., Ph.D.

Dunne, Pamela Darranger. *The Creative Therapeutic Thinker.* Encino, Ca. Center for Psychological Change, 1990.

Bergren, Mark, Cox, Molly, & Detmar, Jim. *Improvise this! How to think on your feet so you don't fall on your face.* Hyperion Press, NY. 2002

Berry, Kathleen *"The Oral Language and Learning of Grade 5 Students."* Unpublished Master's thesis, University of Alberta, 1982.

Blair, Rhonda. Liberating the Young Actor: Feminist Pedagogy and Performance. *Theatre Topics*, Vol. 2, No.1, 1992.

Blatner, Adam, Ed. with Daniel J. Wiener. *Interactive and Improvisational Drama. Varieties of Applied Theatre and Performance,* Lincoln, NE., iUniverse, 2007.

Bolton, Gavin. *Drama as Education: An Argument for Placing Drama at the Centre of the Curriculum.* London. Longman, 1984.

Bolton, Gavin. *Toward a Theory of Drama in Education.* London: Longman, 1979.

Booth, David. *Story Drama*. Markham. ON. Pembroke Publishers, 1994.

Booth, Eric. *The everyday work of art: Awakening the extraordinary in your daily life.* Lincoln, NE., iuniverse, 2001.

Brecht, Bertolt. *Brecht on Theatre.* translated by John Willett. New York. Hill and Wang, 1964

Britton, James. *Language and Learning.* Harmondsworth, Mdsx: Penguin, 1970.

Cameron, Julia. *Walking in this world: The practiced art of creativity.* New York: Penguin Putnam., 2002

Case, Sue-Ellen. *Feminism and Theatre.* London, MacMillan, 1988.

Davis, Tracy C. *A Doll's House and the Evolving Feminist Agenda: A Feminist Research Prospect and Retrospect.* ed. Peta Tancred-Sheriff. McGill Queen's University Press, 1988.

Dell, Paul F. Violence and the Systemic View: The Problem of Power. *Family Process*, Vol. 28, No.1, 1-14. Family Process, Inc., 1989.

Dolan, Jill. *The Feminist Spectator as Critic*. Ann Arbor. UMI, 1988.

Ellis, Mary Lynne. "Women: The Mirage of the Perfect Image. *The Arts in Psychotherapy*. Vol. 16, No.4, 263-276. Pergamon Press, 1989.

Field, Syd. *Screenplay: The Foundations of Screenwriting*. New York. Dell Publishing, 1982.

Fukuyama, Francis. *The End of History and the Last Man*. New York: Avon Books, 1993.

Fulwiler, Toby. Journals across the Disciplines. Urbana, Ill. *English Journal*, National Council of Teachers of English, Vol. 69, No. 9, pps 14-19, Dec., 1980.

Gold, Muriel. The Fictional Family: A Perspective of Many Cultures. *English Quarterly* 25.2 (Spring, 1993): 26-29.

Gold, Muriel. The Fictional Family in Actor Training. *Speech and Drama*, 37(2),9-18. Oxford: Society of Teachers of Speech and Drama, 1988.

Gold, Muriel. *The Fictional Family: In Drama, Education and Groupwork*. Springfield, Ill. Charles C Thomas, 1991.

Gold, Muriel. The Fictional Family Approach: Dramatic Techniques for Family Therapy Trainees. *Contaminating Theatre. Intersections of theatre, therapy, and public health*. MacDougall, Jill and P. Stanley Yoder, Evanston, Ill., 1998.

Gold, Muriel. *Therapy Through Drama: The Fictional Family*. Springfield, Ill. Charles C Thomas, 2000

Gold, Muriel. The Fictional Family in Drama and Across the Curriculum, Blatner, Adam, Ed. with Daniel J. Wiener. *Interactive and Improvisational Drama. Varieties of Applied Theatre and Performance*, Lincoln, NE., iUniverse, 2007.

Gressler, Thomas H. *Theatre as the essential liberal art in the American university.* Lewiston, N.Y., Edwin Mellen Press, 2002

Harrop, John and Sabin Epstein. *Acting with Style.* Prentice-Hall. Englewood Cliffs, New Jersey, 1982.

Heathcote, Dorothy and Gavin Bolton. *Drama for Learning.* Portsmouth, NH. Heinemann, 1995.

Heathcote, Dorothy. Learning, Knowing, and Languaging in Drama: An Interview with Dorothy Heathcote. *Language Arts*, 60, 6, 695-701, 1983.

Heathcote, Dorothy. *Three Looms Waiting.* BBC Television production, 1971.

Hodgson, John and Ernest Richards. *Improvisation.* London. Methuen and Company, 1969.

Jent, Deanna Banz. *Sex Roles in the Acting Class: Exploring the Effects of Actor Training on Nonverbal Gender Display,* Doctoral dissertation, Evanston: 1989.

Johnson, Liz, and Cecily O'Neill (Eds.). *Dorothy Heathcote: Collected Writings on Education and Drama.* London: Hutchison, 1984.

Johnston, Chris. *The Improvisation Game: discovering the secrets of spontaneous performance.* London: Nick Hern, 2006.

Koch, Kenneth. *Wishes, Lies, and Dreams.* New York. Vintage Books/ Chelsea House Publishers, 1970

Kerrigan, Sheila. *The performer's guide to the collaborative process.* Portsmouth, NH: Heinemann, 2001.

LaCapra, Dominick. *History and Criticism.* Ithaca: Cornell University Press, 1985.

LaCapra, Dominick and Steven L. Kaplan. (eds.) *Modern European Intellectual History.* Ithaca: Cornell University Press, 1982.

Laird, Joan. Women and Ritual in Family Therapy. *In* Evan Imber-Black, Janine Roberts and Richard Whiting (Eds.). *Rituals in*

Families and Family Therapy. New York: W. W. Norton & Company, 1988.

Landy, Robert. *Drama Therapy: concepts and practices.* Springfield, Ill. Charles C Thomas, 1985

Lowe, Robert. *Improvisation, Inc.: Harnessing spontaneity to engage people and groups.* San Francisco: Jossey-Bass, 2000.

McGoldrick, Monica. (1982). Normal Families: An Ethnic Perspective. In Froma Walsh,(Ed.). *Normal Family Processes*: The Guilford Press.

McGoldrick, Monica and Elizabeth A. Carter. The Family Life Cycle. *In* Froma Walsh (Ed.). *Normal Family Processes*. New York: The Guilford Press, 1982.

Mallett, Margaret, and Newsome, Bernard. *Talking, Writing, and Learning* 8-13. London: Evans/Methuen Educational, 1970.

Moore, Sonia. *The Stanislavski System.* New York. Penguin Books, 1987

Morgan, Norah, and Saxton, Juliana. *Teaching Drama*. London: Hutchison, 1987.

Nelson, Linda & Finneran, Lanell. *Drama and the adolescent journey: warm-ups and activities to address teen issues*. Portsmouth, NH: Heinemann, 2006.

Nietzsche, Friedrich. *Untimely Meditations*. Cambridge: Cambridge University Press, 1997.

O'Neill, Cecily. *Process Drama*. Portsmouth, NH. Heinemann, 1995.

O'Neill, Cecily, and Alan Lambert. *Drama Structures*. London: Hutchison, 1984..

Powell, Brian. *English Through Poetry Writing.* London. Heinemann Educational   Books Ltd., 1968

Price, Sharon and Patrick McHenry. *Divorce*. Sage, 1988.

Searle, Dennis. *The Language of Adolescents In and Out of School.* Unpublished doctoral dissertation, University of London, 1981.

Shurtleff, Michael. *Audition.* New York. Walker & Co., 1978.

Siegel, Marilyn. *Exploratory Study of the Long-Tern Unattached* unpublished doctoral thesis, McGill University, Montreal,1989

Skynner, Robin and John Cleese (1984). *Families and how to survive them.* New York, Oxford University Press.

Stanislavski, Constantin. *Creating a Role.* translated by Elisabeth Hapgood. New York. Theatre Arts, 1961.

Sternberg, Pat & Garcia, Antonina. *Who's in your shoes?* (2nd ed.) Westport, CT: Praeger, 2000.

Strongylu, Nina. Cultural Identity & Gender. *Dramascope*, Vol. X, No. 1, 9-10, 1990.

Taylor, Philip & Warner. *Structure and spontaneity: the drama in education of Cecily O'Neill.* Sterling, VA: Stylus, 2006.

Todd, Susan. *Women & Theatre: Calling the Shots.* London: Faber & Faber, 1984.

Verriour, Patrick, and Carol Tarlington. *Role Drama.* Markham, ON: Pembroke Publishers, 1991

Vygotsky, Lev. *Language and Thought.* Cambridge, MA: MIT Press, 1962

Wagner, Betty Jane. Dorothy Heathcote: *Drama as a Learning Medium.* Washington, DC. National Education Association, 1976.

Walsh, Froma. The family in later life. In E.A. Carter & M. McGoldrick (Eds.). *The Family Life Cycle: A Framework for Family Therapy.* New York: Gardner Press, 1980.

Wilcoxon, S. Allen. Contemporary Developments in Marital and Family Therapy. *Family Therapy*, Vol. XVI, No.1, 87-94 San Diego: Libra Publishers, Inc., 1989.

Willett, John. (Ed.) (1964). *Brecht on Theatre*. New York: Hill and Wang.

_____. *Mind in Society*. Cambridge, MA: Harvard University Press, 1978.

Index

feminism 150, 155, 157
Field, Syd 10, 83, 98, 205
Fillion, Bryant xviii
Fukuyama, Francis 115, 129, 130, 205
Fulwiler, Toby xviii, 92, 93, 98, 205
Future projection 173

G

Games 18
Gardner, Howard xx, 117, 130, 178, 208
gender x, xxii, 47, 119, 148, 149, 154, 162, 164, 166, 167, 168, 169, 170, 171, 173, 177, 215
geography xxiii, 44, 45, 195
gestus 18, 19, 22, 110
Grinder, John 13, 27, 203
Group Dynamics 24, 79
Group Encounter 173
group solidarity 5

H

Hansberry, Lorraine 137
Harrop, John 18, 27, 206
Healy, Mary xviii, 73, 203
Heathcote, Dorothy ix, x, xiii, xvii, 26, 27, 30, 40, 49, 50, 183, 201, 206, 208
Hébert, Anne vii, xv
History Curriculum 114
Hodgson, John 2, 9, 27, 206
Holocaust 55, 58, 59, 216
Houses 15, 42, 161, 182, 199

I

Ibsen, Henrik xxii, 162, 163, 164, 166
immigration 55
improvisation ix, 8, 9, 13, 17, 20, 30, 37, 60, 76, 82, 83, 89, 144, 181, 189
inner monologues xix, 15, 26, 94, 95, 97, 139, 142, 171
Interdisciplinary 46

intervention 80, 96, 171, 174, 196

J

Jewish Literature 55
Johnson, Liz 40, 49, 206
journals xix, 10, 11, 22, 62, 70, 91, 92, 93, 95, 97, 100, 141, 145, 175

K

Kaplan, Steven L. 129, 130, 206
Koch, Kenneth 100, 102, 110, 113, 206

L

LaCapra, Dominick 129, 130, 206
Landy, Robert xxv, 84, 98, 147, 207
language arts xvii, xviii, 26, 29, 43, 47
lesbianism xxii, 154, 159
literature teaching xxi, 132
logocentrism 115

M

Mallett, Margaret 39, 49, 207
Marx 127
masks 18, 20, 84
Mathematics 45
McGoldrick, Monica 54, 146, 147, 157, 178, 207, 208
Moore, Sonia 3, 9, 27, 95, 98, 207
moral and religious education xviii, 29, 145
Morgan, Norah 40, 49, 207
multicultural education x, xxi, 131, 132
Multicultural Grouping 134
Multiple Intelligence Theory xx, 117

N

Narrative Essay 64
Nazi 58, 121
Newsome, Bernard 39, 49, 207

Verriour, Patrick 40, 50, 208
visualization xix, 2, 78, 97, 139
Vygotsky, Lev xii, xiii, 31, 50, 208

W

Way, Brian 9, 98
Willett, John 27, 147, 204, 209
Writing across the Curriculum 51

Contributors

DAVID DILLON, Ph.D. is Professor in the Faculty of Education at McGill University in Montreal. After beginning his work in education as a teacher, his career has been in teacher education at the University of Alberta (1977-89) and McGill University (1989-present). However, he has also served as editor (*Language Arts*, 1983-1090, and *English Quarterly*, 1990-1995), developer of literature-based instructional kits for literacy for Scholastic Canada, and advisor to the Ministry of Education *via* membership on the Quebec Superior Council of Education (2001-2004). Most recently, he has been exploring more extensive school-based approaches for preparing future teachers, including the teaching of drama.

MURIEL GOLD, C.M., Ph.D., theatre producer/director, educator and writer, is former Artistic Director of The Saidye Bronfman Centre Theatre in Montreal. She has conducted workshops with secondary school drama teachers, and has presented collective creations based on her Fictional Family technique both with professional actors and with graduate students. Dr. Gold has given workshops and lectures on the multiple uses of the Fictional Family technique (in actor training, drama in education, multi-cultural awareness, gender awareness) to Canadian & U.S. universities and professional organizations. She is the author of several books, including *THE FICTIONAL FAMILY in Drama, Education and Groupwork,* 1991, and *Therapy Through Drama: The Fictional Family,* 2000. The latter has been used as a text for graduate drama therapy students. Other books by Dr. Gold are: *Tell Me Why Nights are Lonesome* (2004), and *A Gift for their Mother: A History of the Saidye Bronfman Centre Theatre,* (2007). Her current book, *The Dramatic Legacy of Dorothy Davis and Violet Walters: The Montreal Children's Theatre 1933-2009,* is in press. In recognition of her lifetime achievement in drama and theatre, she was appointed a Member of the Order of Canada.

JUDITH KALMAN, M.A. (deceased) taught composition and business communication in both the department of English and the department of Marketing at Concordia University in Montreal, and English literature at Dawson College in Montreal, where she developed a course in Holocaust Literature. She has given workshops and published articles on various writing techniques and writing problems, including both critical thinking and an adaptation of Muriel Gold's Fictional Family technique in the writing classroom, the literature classroom, and the business classroom.

SAMUEL KALMAN, Ph.D. is an Assistant Professor in History at St. Francis Xavier University, Canada. He received his doctorate from McMaster University (thesis topic: The concepts of the nation and the state in the doctrines of the *Faisceau* and the *Croix de Feu/Parti social francais,* two prominent extreme-rightist leagues in interwar France). He is the author of *The extreme right in interwar France: The Faisceau and the Croix du feu,* Ashgate Publishing Ltd., 2008

MICHAEL SOMMERS, M.A. was born in Texas and grew up in Toronto, Canada. After graduating from McGill University with a B.A. in Literature, he moved to Paris, France where he became a journalist and received a Masters in History and Civilizations from the Ecole des

Hautes Etudes en Sciences Sociales (thesis topic: "The Image of Brazil and Brazilians in Hollywood Cinema.") Aside from Paris, he has lived for long periods in New York and Lisbon. He has lived in Salvador, Brazil, for the past eight years, and is author of the Moon Series Travel Guides.

CECILIA UGARTE, B.A. is a graduate of the Dawson College Illustration and Design program. She also holds a Bachelor of Arts from McGill University. Her other published illustrated works include Muriel Gold's "A Gift for their Mother", and a plethora of school curriculum books with the Jewish Educational Council. She presently lives with her husband, Charles, and their two children, Selina Michelle and Julian Joseph, in Ile Bizard, Quebec.